THE OFFICIAL BETTER BRIDGE SERIES

BRIDGE BASICS 3

Popular Conventions

Audrey Grant

D1053919

Published by
Baron Barclay

Bridge Basics 3: Popular Conventions
Copyright © 2007 Audrey Grant's Better Bridge Inc.

If you'd like to contact the author, see page 229.

Baron Barclay
3600 Chamberlain Lane, Suite 206
Louisville, KY 40241
U.S. and Canada: 1-800-274-2221
Worldwide: 502-426-0410
FAX: 502-426-2044
www.baronbarclay.com

ISBN-10: 0-939460-92-0
ISBN-13: 978-0-939460-92-2

Illustrations by Kelvin Smith
Design and composition by John Reinhardt Book Design

Printed in the United States of America

Contents

Contents

The Bridge Basics Series

The Improving Your Judgment Series

... more to come

Introduction

The BRIDGE BASICS SERIES uses Audrey Grant Standard, a modern approach that is played in most games among friends playing at home, in golf clubs, in bridge clubs, onboard ships, and online. The Advisory Committee for this system includes the best players in the world.

BRIDGE BASICS 3–POPULAR CONVENTIONS covers the information needed to understand basic conventions. These are artificial calls that have a defined meaning. A key to success is to become completely familiar with the few conventions that will be most useful in helping you play better bridge. The caution is to avoid too many unnatural bids; they may be more confusing than helpful. Famous author and world champion, Bill Root, wrote, "It is far better to play a few conventions well than a great many conventions erratically." Quality must come before quantity.

In this book, we've selected a few popular, basic, widely-used conventions that are part of the framework of the game. The goal is to carefully illustrate the problem that these bids are designed to solve, and to present enough detail that you will be comfortable adding these conventions to your bidding system.

The best way to absorb information is to use it. The thirty-two carefully prepared deals in this book provide the chance to practice. They put the bidding into a meaningful context and advance our play of the hand and defensive skills. Color-coded Cards are available to simplify dealing the hands (see next page).

Some players agree to play a convention and then hope that it doesn't come up! When you've finished reading this book and playing the practice deals, I'm confident that you'll be looking forward to using these conventions to help you reach the best contract.

All the best,
Audrey Grant
www.AudreyGrant.com

Audrey's Coded Cards

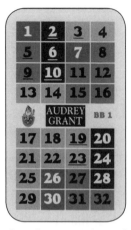

For each Better Bridge book in the Basic series there is a companion deck of color-coded cards available (see page 230), designed to make it easy to deal and play all thirty-two practice deals.

To use the cards, place the guide card that accompanies the deck in the center of the table.

Distribute each of the cards according to the color-coding on the back. To

distribute Deal #7, for example, look at the box numbered 7 on the back of each card. If the box is red, the card goes to North; if it is blue, the card goes to East; yellow goes to South; green goes to West.

Check that each player has thirteen cards with the appropriate color on the back. If you are North on Deal #7, for example, all your

cards should have a red background in box #7. The dealer is indicated by an underline of the number in the box. It is also indicated on the guide card. The deal is then ready to be bid and played, and replayed, as often as desired.

If you are practicing by yourself, turn all four hands face up on the table, dummy style, and walk through the bidding and play, using the text as a guide where necessary.

If you don't have the color-coded cards available, sort a deck of cards into suits and construct the four hands one suit at a time.

The carefully constructed deals are designed as a practical tool to improve your comfort with popular conventions.

Acknowledgments

To my husband, *David Lindop*, a world-class player who works hand-in-hand with me to produce the bridge books.

To *Jason Grant-Lindop* and *Joanna Grant* for their support and involvement in the many aspects of Better Bridge

To the Better Bridge Advisory Committee:

- *Henry Francis*—Member of the Bridge Hall of Fame, Editor of the Official Encyclopedia of Bridge
- *Fred Gitelman*—Founder of Bridge Base Inc., gold medalist
- *Bob Hamman*—World Champion, top-ranked male player
- *Petra Hamman*—World Champion, bridge teacher
- *Jerry Helms*—Professional bridge teacher and player
- *Shawn Quinn*—World Champion, top-ranked female player

To Robert Williams, Associate Dean Emeritus, N.C. State University, for his help in editing the book.

To the bridge teachers. Your dedication, skill, and professionalism have made me proud to be counted among you.

To the students of the game—thank you for sharing your ideas and your enthusiasm.

When the bidding starts with 1NT, there is a comfortable smoothness about the auction. But this very ease should not lull the partnership to a final notrump contract, willy-nilly. Indeed, the hands may play better in a major suit.

—Sam Stayman, The Complete Stayman System of Contract Bidding (1956)

The Stayman Convention

The Stayman convention is used by *responder* after a notrump opening bid. To understand the use of Stayman we need to start by reviewing the requirements for a 1NT opening and responder's decisions when partner opens 1NT.

The 1NT Opening Bid

The 1NT opening bid is very descriptive. It shows:

> ### Opening 1NT Bid
>
> - 15, 16, or 17 valuation points.
> - A balanced hand

Valuation points for an opening bid are a combination of *high-card points (HCPs)* and *length points*. A *balanced hand* has no *voids*, no *singletons*, and at most one *doubleton*. So all three of these hands would qualify for a 1NT opening bid:

1. A hand with one four-card suit and three three-card suits (4-3-3-3 *distribution*):

♠ K J 5
♥ A Q 7 3
♦ Q 10 4
♣ K 9 5

This hand has 15 high-card points and balanced distribution.

2. A hand with two four-card suits, a three-card suit, and a doubleton (4-4-3-2):

♠ A Q 8 4
♥ 8 3
♦ K Q 5
♣ A J 6 2

There are 16 high-card points and the hand is balanced. You don't need high cards in every suit to open 1NT.

3. A hand with one five-card suit, two three-card suits, and a doubleton (5-3-3-2):

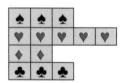

♠ Q J 5
♥ K 10 9 7 5
♦ A Q
♣ K J 7

There are 16 high-card points plus 1 length point for the five-card heart suit[1], for a total of 17 valuation points. Open 1NT even with a five-card major suit.

With a balanced hand too weak (12–14) or too strong (18–19) to open 1NT, open one of a suit[2].

---

[1] Some players prefer to count only high card points for valuation when opening 1NT.

[2] Opening with balanced hands of 20 or more points is discussed in Chapter 3.

Responding to a 1NT Opening Bid

The opening 1NT bid is so descriptive that responder is usually well-placed to decide both How High and Where the partnership belongs.

Deciding How High

About 25–26 combined points are needed for *game* in notrump or a major suit, so this is a matter of addition:

- If responder has 0–7 points, the partnership belongs in *partscore*. If both opener and responder have the top of the range, there are at most 24 combined points (17 + 7).
- If responder has 8–9 points, there may be a game. If both opener and responder have the bottom of the range, there are only 23 combined points (15 + 8). If they both have the top of their range, there are 26 combined points (17 + 9).
- If responder has 10–15 points, the partnership belongs in game. Even if both opener and responder have the bottom of the range, there are at least 25 combined points (15 + 10).
- If responder has 16 or more points, there may be a *slam*. More on this in Chapter 4.

Deciding Where

Ideally, the partnership wants to play in an eight-card or longer trump *fit*. However, the decision on Where to play depends on How High:

If the partnership belongs in partscore:

- When responder has a five-card or longer suit, responder generally chooses to play partscore in the trump suit.

If the partnership belongs in game:

- When there is an eight-card or longer *major suit* fit, responder generally chooses to play in the major; **otherwise, responder usually chooses to play in 3NT**, since 5♣ and 5♦ require eleven tricks.

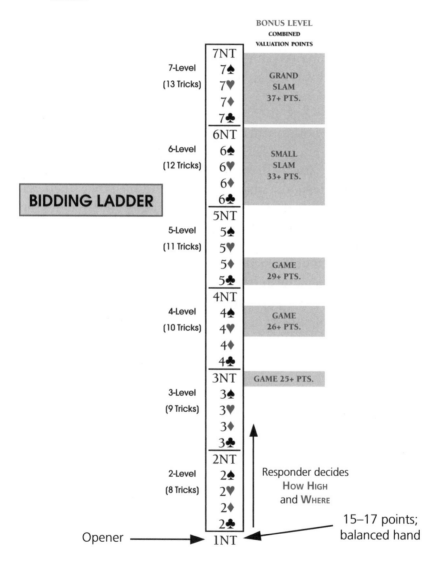

When Responder Knows How High and Where

WHEN THE PARTNERSHIP BELONGS IN PARTSCORE

With 0–7 points, responder knows the partnership belongs at the partscore level and can decide on the best contract.

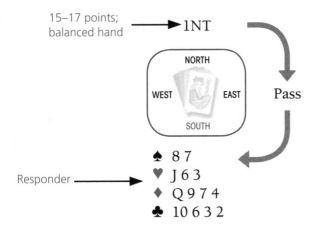

15–17 points;
balanced hand ——▶ 1NT

Pass

Responder ——▶

♠ 8 7
♥ J 6 3
♦ Q 9 7 4
♣ 10 6 3 2

How High? Partscore. With 3 high-card points, responder knows there are at most 20 combined points (17 + 3).

Where? With no five-card or longer suit, responder chooses to play in notrump. There could be an eight-card fit, but there is not enough room to explore and still stop at a low level in partscore.

Decision: Pass. This will leave opener to play partscore in 1NT.

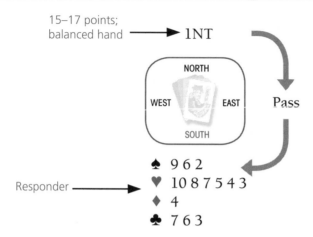

15–17 points;
balanced hand ⟶ 1NT

NORTH

WEST   EAST   Pass

SOUTH

Responder ⟶

♠ 9 6 2
♥ 10 8 7 5 4 3
♦ 4
♣ 7 6 3

How High? Partscore. With no high-card points and 2 length points for the six-card heart suit, responder knows there are at most 19 combined points (17 + 2).

Where? Hearts. Since opener's balanced hand shows at least two hearts, responder knows the partnership has an eight-card or longer heart fit.

Decision: Partscore in 2♥. The classic way for responder to put the partnership in a partscore at the two level is to simply bid the suit[3], 2♥. This is a *signoff* bid which opener is expected to pass. A different method of signing off in 2♥ is discussed in Chapter 2, but the key is that responder doesn't need any high-card strength to remove the partnership from 1NT and put it in a partscore in a trump suit.

---

[3] Responses of 2♦, 2♥, and 2♠, are signoff bids. 2♣ is reserved for the Stayman convention, introduced later in this chapter.

WHEN THE PARTNERSHIP BELONGS IN GAME

With 10–15 points, responder knows the partnership belongs at the game level and can often decide on the best contract with no further information from opener.

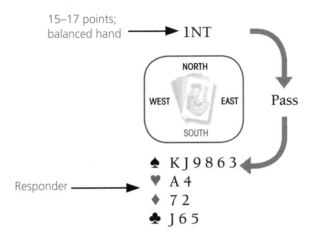

How High? Game. With 9 high-card points plus 2 length points for the six-card spade suit, responder knows there are at least 26 combined points (15 + 11).

Where? Spades. Opener has at least two spades, so the partnership has an eight-card spade fit.

Decision: Game in 4♠. The classic way for responder to put the partnership in game in a major suit is to simply jump to the game level, 4♠. This is a signoff bid. A different way to put the partnership in 4♠ will be discussed in Chapter 2, but the key is that responder knows both **How High** and **Where** the partnership belongs.

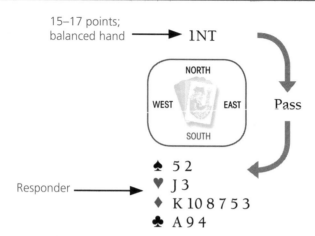

15–17 points;
balanced hand ⟶ 1NT

NORTH

WEST   EAST   Pass

SOUTH

♠ 5 2
Responder ⟶ ♥ J 3
♦ K 10 8 7 5 3
♣ A 9 4

How High? Game. Responder has 8 high-card points and 2 length points for the six-card diamond suit. So, responder knows there are at least 25 combined points (15 + 10).

Where? Notrump. Although the partnership must have at least an eight-card fit in diamonds, when it comes to **Where**, responder chooses game in notrump rather than diamonds. It should be easier to take nine tricks in 3NT than eleven tricks in 5♦.

Decision: 3NT. Note that, although opener needs a balanced hand to open 1NT, responder doesn't need a balanced hand to put the partnership in 3NT.

Examples When Responder Needs More Information

Responder sometimes needs help from opener to decide How HIGH. With 8 or 9 points, responder can't be sure if there is enough combined strength for game.

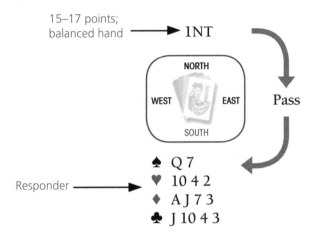

How HIGH? Partscore or game? With 8 high-card points, responder is unsure about How HIGH. If opener is at the minimum of the notrump range, 15 points, there are at most 23 combined points (15 + 8) and the partnership belongs in partscore; if opener has 17 points, there will be 25 combined points (17 + 8), enough to go for a contract of 3NT.

WHERE? Notrump. Since there is unlikely to be an eight-card major suit fit[4], responder knows the partnership belongs in notrump.

DECISION: 2NT. To get further information from opener, responder makes an *invitational* raise to 2NT. Opener can pass and stop in partscore with a minimum or continue to game with the top of the range.

---

[4] Opener could have opened 1NT with a five-card heart suit, but it is usually practical to ignore that possibility.

Responder may also need help from opener to decide **WHERE**:

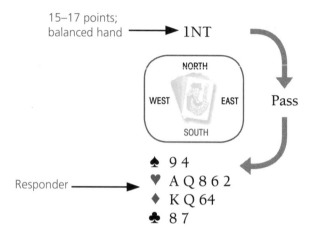

15–17 points;
balanced hand ────▶ 1NT

NORTH

WEST   EAST   Pass

SOUTH

♠ 9 4
Responder ────▶ ♥ A Q 8 6 2
♦ K Q 64
♣ 8 7

HOW HIGH? Game. With 11 high-card points plus 1 length point for the five-card heart suit, responder knows there are at least 27 combined points (15 + 12).

WHERE? Notrump or hearts? If opener has only two hearts, the best contract is likely to be 3NT; if opener has three or more hearts, the partnership has an eight-card fit and likely belongs in 4♥.

DECISION: Responder needs to make a *forcing* bid that asks opener to choose 3NT with only two hearts or 4♥ with three-card or longer heart *support*. The classic way to do this is for responder to jump to 3♥. In Chapter 2 we will see another way to handle this type of hand.

Now, let's consider one more hand for responder.

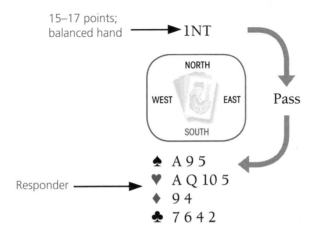

15–17 points; balanced hand ⟶ 1NT

NORTH

WEST | EAST | Pass

SOUTH

Responder ⟶
♠ A 9 5
♥ A Q 10 5
♦ 9 4
♣ 7 6 4 2

How High? Game. With 10 high-card points, responder knows there are at least 25 combined points (15 + 10), enough to go for a game contract.

Where? Notrump or hearts? If opener has four hearts, the partnership has an eight-card major suit fit and belongs in 4♥; if not, the partnership belongs in 3NT.

Decision: With a balanced hand like this, it might seem best to simply ignore the possibility of an eight-card fit in hearts and go for the nine-trick game in 3NT. Four-four (4-4) fits, however, have excellent trick-taking potential. So, before we see how responder can find out if opener has four hearts, let's take a look at an example of the advantages of playing in a 4-4 major suit fit.

The Importance of the 4-4 Major Suit Fit

Nine tricks are needed to make 3NT; ten tricks are needed to make 4♥ or 4♠. Yet it is usually preferable to play game in the major suit when there is an eight-card or longer fit. To see why, consider the following deal where South opens 1NT and North has enough strength to take the partnership to the game level:

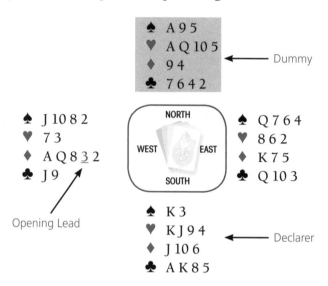

First, suppose North puts the partnership in 3NT, the nine-trick game. If West leads the ♦3, *fourth highest* from longest and strongest, the defenders immediately take the first five diamond tricks to defeat the contract. Even if West did not lead a diamond initially, the defenders would get a second chance. Declarer, South, has only eight *winners* in a notrump contract: two spades, four hearts, and two clubs. To develop a ninth trick, declarer would have to use the length in the club suit. South could play the ♣A, ♣K, and give up a trick to East's ♣Q. South's remaining club would be a winner, but the defenders would have another opportunity to take their winners in the diamond suit.

3NT could be defeated even if the defenders' diamonds were divided 4-4 instead of 5-3. The opponents could take only four diamond tricks, but declarer couldn't make the contract without giving up a club trick, and that would be the fifth trick for the defenders.

Now let's consider what would happen if South is declarer in a 4♥ contract. One more trick is required, but there are three advantages to playing in the 4-4 heart fit on this deal.

1. Having a trump suit prevents the defenders from taking tricks in their long suit. The defenders can take only two diamond tricks. If they lead a third round, declarer can *ruff* with one of dummy's hearts.
2. Declarer can get an extra trick from the 4-4 trump fit. In notrump, declarer can get only four winners from the heart suit. With hearts as the trump suit, declarer will get **five** heart tricks. Declarer can ruff a diamond with one of dummy's hearts and still take four tricks with South's hearts[5]. If North held a singleton diamond, South might gain two tricks by ruffing diamonds twice in the dummy.
3. Declarer can afford to give up the lead while developing tricks without being concerned that the defenders can take too many established winners in their long suit. After drawing the defenders' trumps on this deal, declarer can play the ♣A-K and a third round of clubs to develop a winner in the suit through length without any fear of the defenders taking all their diamond winners. Declarer still has a trump left.

So, declarer will make a contract of 4♥ on these combined hands. The only tricks the defenders will take are two diamonds and a club. Playing with hearts as the trump suit allows declarer to take **two** more tricks on this deal than playing in a notrump contract.

[5] Alternatively, declarer could trump the third round of spades in the South hand and take four heart tricks with North's trumps. An advantage of playing in a 4-4 trump fit is that declarer can gain a trick by ruffing in *either* hand.

Although it isn't always the case, playing in an eight-card or longer major suit fit will usually provide at least one more trick than playing in a notrump contract, and sometimes two or more tricks.

What about looking for eight-card or longer *minor suit* fits if there is no potential major suit fit? Unfortunately, a contract of 5♣ or 5♦ requires two more tricks than a contract of 3NT, so it will rarely be a better contract. When going for a game contract, it is usually better for responder to ignore length in a minor suit, even with an *unbalanced* hand, and go for the nine-trick game in 3NT. On this deal, for example, North and South can't make a 5♣ contract despite the 4-4 club fit. The defenders will get three tricks: two diamonds and a club.

So, what forcing bid can responder use to uncover the 4-4 heart fit after South opens 1NT on this deal? Responder can't bid 2♥ because that would be a signoff bid and opener would pass. A jump to 3♥ asks opener to bid 4♥ with three-card or longer support. Another approach is needed.

The Stayman Convention

In 1945, Sam Stayman of New York published an article in THE
BRIDGE WORLD which suggested that when partner opens 1NT, a
response of 2♣ can be used to ask whether opener holds a four-card
major suit. This idea quickly became popular and is known as the
Stayman convention[6].

The essential requirements for responder to use the Stayman
convention are:

Using the 2♣ (Stayman) Convention

- At least one four-card major suit.
- 8+ points[7].

The 2♣ response is referred to as a *conventional bid*. It is totally artificial,
having nothing to do with suggesting clubs as a possible trump suit.
The 1NT opener replies to the Stayman inquiry as follows:

1NT Opener's Reply to the 2♣ (Stayman) Convention

- 2♠   Four-card or longer spade suit.
- 2♥   Four-card or longer heart suit.*
- 2♦   No four-card or longer major suit.

* With four hearts and four spades, opener bids 2♥,
bidding "up the line."

Like the conventional 2♣ response, opener's 2♦ reply to show
no major suit has nothing to do with diamonds. It is entirely
artificial.

---

[6] The idea was originally suggested to Stayman by his partner, George Rapee, but it was
Stayman who actively developed, published, and promoted the idea. Other players, including
Ewart Kempson, S. J. Simon, and John Marx, had worked on the concept, but it is universally
known as "Stayman."

[7] See exception on page 28.

Examples of Opener's Reply to the Stayman Convention

After opening 1NT and hearing a 2♣ response from partner, opener's reply is automatic. Here are some examples after opener has bid 1NT and responder has bid 2♣.

	OPENER	RESPONDER	
	1NT	2♣	←——— Stayman
	?		

♠ K Q 8
♥ A J 10
♦ J 3
♣ K Q 8 7 3

2♦. With no four-card major, opener replies 2♦ to responder's 2♣ bid. The 2♦ reply has nothing to do with opener's holding in diamonds or whether opener is at the top or bottom of the 1NT range.

♠ A K 10
♥ 9 7 5 2
♦ Q 7 3
♣ A Q 5

2♥. With a four-card heart suit, opener replies 2♥. The strength of the heart suit doesn't matter. All opener is telling responder is that opener holds four hearts.

♠ A Q 9 6
♥ K 10 7 3
♦ A 9
♣ Q 8 4

2♥. With both major suits, opener bids 2♥[8].

♠ A J 8 7 3
♥ K J
♦ Q J 5
♣ K 10 7

2♠. A reply of 2♠ by opener shows a four-card or longer spade suit. Responder will assume opener has only a four-card spade suit and the partnership will sometimes miss an eight-card fit, but it will not usually be a problem.

---

[8] Some partnerships prefer to reply 2♠ with both major suits or to bid the stronger of the two suits, but this is not standard practice.

Using the Stayman Convention

Let's see how the Stayman convention would be used on the earlier deal.

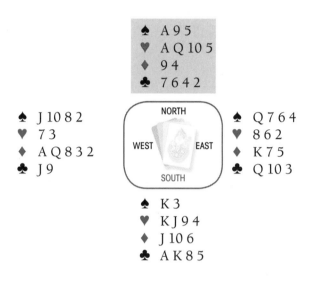

	♠ A 9 5	
	♥ A Q 10 5	
	♦ 9 4	
	♣ 7 6 4 2	

♠ J 10 8 2   ♠ Q 7 6 4
♥ 7 3   ♥ 8 6 2
♦ A Q 8 3 2   ♦ K 7 5
♣ J 9   ♣ Q 10 3

♠ K 3
♥ K J 9 4
♦ J 10 6
♣ A K 8 5

WEST	NORTH (RESPONDER)	EAST	SOUTH (OPENER)
			1NT
Pass	2♣	Pass	2♥
Pass	4♥	Pass	Pass
Pass			

After South opens 1NT, North's hand meets the requirements for using the Stayman convention: a four-card heart suit and 10 high-card points. The 2♣ response is artificial and forcing. South's reply of 2♥ promises a four-card or longer heart suit. Now responder has the answer to both How High—game—and Where—hearts. North has enough information to place the contract in 4♥. Opener respects responder's decision and passes.

Let's look at more examples of how responder can make use of the 2♣ response to get the partnership to the best contract.

Using Stayman with a Game-Going Hand (10–15 Points)

With 10–15 points[9], responder has the answer to How High, game. The only question is Where? With at least one four-card major suit, responder uses the Stayman convention and decides Where to place the contract after hearing opener's reply. Here are examples for responder after partner opens 1NT.

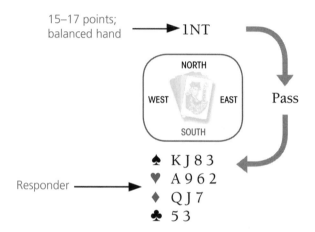

15–17 points; balanced hand ⟶ 1NT

NORTH

WEST   EAST   Pass

SOUTH

Responder ⟶

♠ K J 8 3
♥ A 9 6 2
♦ Q J 7
♣ 5 3

2♣. With 11 high-card points, responder knows there are at least 26 combined points (15 + 11), enough for game. With the possibility of a major suit fit in either hearts or spades, responder starts with 2♣. If opener bids 2♥, responder knows the partnership has an eight-card heart fit and puts the partnership in game in 4♥. Similarly, if opener bids 2♠, responder jumps to 4♠. If opener bids 2♦, responder knows there is no eight-card major suit fit and places the contract in 3NT.

---

[9] With 16 or more points, responder is interested in investigating a slam contract. Slam bidding is discussed in Chapter 4.

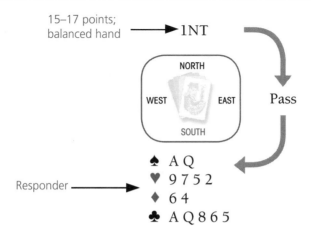

15–17 points;
balanced hand → 1NT

NORTH

WEST   EAST   Pass

SOUTH

Responder →

♠ A Q
♥ 9 7 5 2
♦ 6 4
♣ A Q 8 6 5

2♣. With 12 high-card points plus 1 length point for the five-card club suit, responder knows the partnership has enough combined strength for game. With a four-card heart suit, responder uses Stayman. The quality of responder's four-card heart suit is not important. If opener bids 2♥, responder *raises* to 4♥. If opener bids 2♦ or 2♠, responder knows there is no major suit fit and jumps to 3NT.

The following examples require a little more thought.

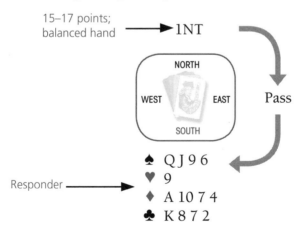

15–17 points;
balanced hand → 1NT

NORTH

WEST   EAST   Pass

SOUTH

Responder →

♠ Q J 9 6
♥ 9
♦ A 10 7 4
♣ K 8 7 2

2♣. With 10 high-card points and a four-card spade suit, responder starts with 2♣. If opener bids 2♠, responder jumps to 4♠, knowing both **How High** and **Where** the partnership belongs. If opener rebids 2♦, responder jumps to 3NT since there is no eight-card major suit fit. Responder doesn't need a balanced hand to put the partnership in a notrump game. If opener bids 2♥, responder again jumps to 3NT on the assumption that there is no major suit fit. It is possible that opener has both four hearts and four spades. If that's the case, opener will now bid 4♠[10]. Since responder didn't raise hearts, opener can infer that responder must have a four-card spade suit to have gone through the Stayman convention on the way to game.

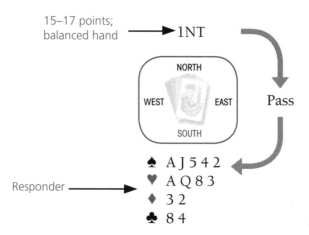

15–17 points; balanced hand ⟶ 1NT

Pass

NORTH
WEST   EAST
SOUTH

Responder ⟶

♠ A J 5 4 2
♥ A Q 8 3
♦ 3 2
♣ 8 4

2♣. With at least one four-card major, responder starts with the Stayman convention. If opener bids 2♥, an eight-card fit has been found and responder raises to 4♥. If opener bids 2♠, a nine-card fit has been found and responder jumps to 4♠. If opener bids 2♦, responder still isn't sure about **Where**. Opener could have three spades. To find out, responder now makes a forcing jump to 3♠, asking opener to bid 3NT with a doubleton spade or 4♠ with three-card support for spades[11].

---

[10] See Practice Deal # 23 for an example.

[11] See Practice Deal # 28 for an example.

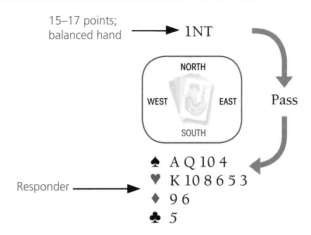

15–17 points;
balanced hand ➔ 1NT

NORTH

WEST   EAST   Pass

SOUTH

♠ A Q 10 4
♥ K 10 8 6 5 3
♦ 9 6
♣ 5

Responder ➔

2♣. Although responder knows there is at least an eight-card fit in hearts, with a four-card spade suit responder starts with 2♣. If opener replies 2♥ or 2♠, a major suit fit has been found and responder can raise to the game level. If opener bids 2♦, responder knows there is no eight-card spade fit and can jump to 4♥, putting the partnership in game in the known heart fit. The reason for going through the Stayman convention is that experience has shown on these types of hands that playing in the 4-4 fit—if there is one—will often produce more tricks than the 6-2, 6-3, or even a 6-4 fit.

Using Stayman with an Invitational Hand (8–9 Points)

The Stayman convention can be used when responder has at least one four-card major suit and an invitational hand of about 8 or 9 points. Responder is unsure about both How High and Where the partnership belongs. Here are some examples after an opening 1NT when responder has an invitational strength hand.

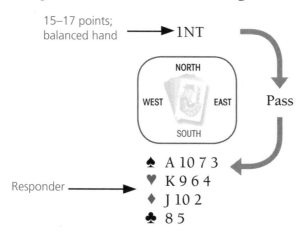

15–17 points; balanced hand ⟶ 1NT

NORTH

WEST   EAST   Pass

SOUTH

Responder ⟶

♠ A 10 7 3
♥ K 9 6 4
♦ J 10 2
♣ 8 5

2♣. With 8 high-card points, responder isn't sure if there is enough combined strength for game. Responder is also unsure whether the partnership has an eight-card major suit fit. To solve both challenges, South starts with Stayman. If opener replies 2♦, showing no major, responder will rebid 2NT, inviting opener to bid 3NT with a maximum. This is similar to raising 1NT to 2NT except that responder has checked for a major suit fit along the way. If opener replies 2♥, responder has uncovered an eight-card heart fit and can invite game by raising to 3♥. Opener can pass with a minimum and continue to game with a maximum. Similarly, if opener replies 2♠, responder will invite game by raising to 3♠.

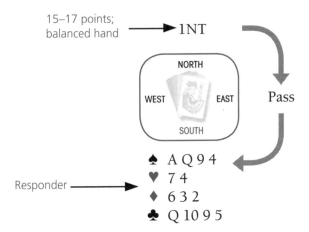

15–17 points; balanced hand ⟶ 1NT

Pass

Responder ⟶
♠ A Q 9 4
♥ 7 4
♦ 6 3 2
♣ Q 10 9 5

2♣. Responder doesn't need both major suits to use Stayman. With 8 high-card points and interest in finding a spade fit, responder starts with 2♣. If opener replies 2♠, responder will make an invitational raise to 3♠. If opener replies 2♦ or 2♥, responder can bid 2NT, inviting opener to game in notrump[12].

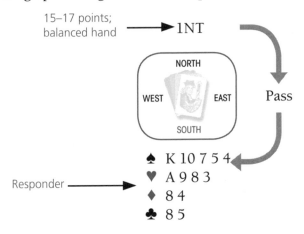

15–17 points; balanced hand ⟶ 1NT

Pass

Responder ⟶
♠ K 10 7 5 4
♥ A 9 8 3
♦ 8 4
♣ 8 5

2♣. South has only 7 high-card points but can add 1 length point for the five-card spade suit. That's enough to be interested in reaching

---

[12] If opener replies 2♥ and also has four spades, opener will infer from the 2NT rebid that responder was interested in spades, not hearts. Opener can now bid 3♠ with a minimum hand and jump to 4♠ with a maximum.

game if opener has a maximum for the 1NT opening. With at least one four-card major, responder starts with 2♣. If opener replies 2♥ or 2♠, responder can invite game by raising to the three level.

If opener replies 2♦, it is still possible there is an eight-card fit in spades if opener has three-card support. Responder can move toward game by bidding 2♠. This shows an invitational hand with five spades. With three-card support, opener can pass with a minimum and jump to 4♠ with a maximum. With a doubleton spade, opener can bid 2NT with a minimum and jump to 3NT with a maximum.

An invitational hand for responder can sometimes become a game-going hand.

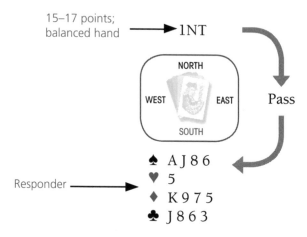

15–17 points; balanced hand ⟶ 1NT

Pass

Responder ⟶

♠ A J 8 6
♥ 5
♦ K 9 7 5
♣ J 8 6 3

2♣. With 9 high-card points and interest in finding a spade fit, South starts with the Stayman convention. If opener replies 2♠, the partnership has an eight-card spade fit and responder is going to be the dummy in a spade contract. Responder can revalue the hand using *dummy points* and the hand becomes worth 12 points: 9 high-card points plus 3 dummy points for the singleton heart. That's enough to take the partnership right to a game contract of 4♠.

If opener replies 2♦ or 2♥, no major suit fit has been found, so the hand is still worth only 9 high-card points. Responder can make an invitational rebid of 2NT.

Other Considerations
for the Stayman Convention

Using Stayman After a Notrump Overcall[13]

The Stayman convention can be used after any natural notrump *overcall*:

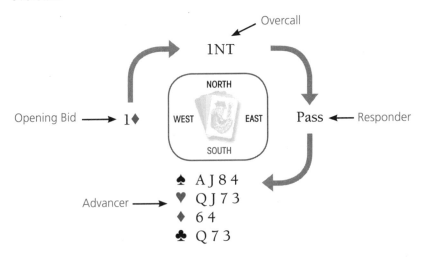

2♣. North's 1NT overcall shows a balanced hand similar to an opening bid of 1NT. South, as *advancer*, can make use of the Stayman convention to look for a major suit fit. If North replies 2♥ or 2♠, South will raise to game in that suit; if North replies 2♦, South will jump to 3NT. If West had opened 1♣, South's 2♣ response to the 1NT overcall would still be the Stayman convention.

---

[13] Chapter 3 discusses using the Stayman convention after an opening bid of 2NT or after a strong 2♣ opening bid and a 2NT or 3NT rebid.

When the notrump opening bid or overcall is at the two level, 3♣ is used as Stayman to ask for a major suit.

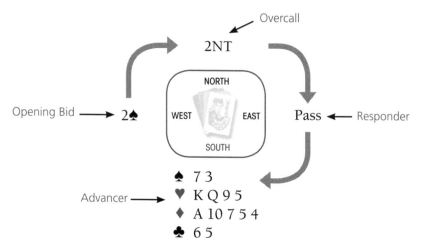

3♣. West's 2♠ opening is a weak two-bid, showing a good six-card suit with about 5–10 points. North's 2NT overcall is natural, showing approximately the equivalent of a 1NT opening bid: a balanced hand with about 15–18 points. As advancer, South can use 3♣[14] as the Stayman convention to see if the partnership has an eight-card heart fit. If North replies 3♥, South can raise to 4♥. If North replies 3♦, South can put the partnership in 3NT.

---

[14] Some partnerships have other understandings in this situation, but this is a popular agreement.

Using Stayman with a Weak Hand (0–7 Points)

With fewer than 8 points, responder does not usually use the Stayman convention. It would risk getting the partnership too high.

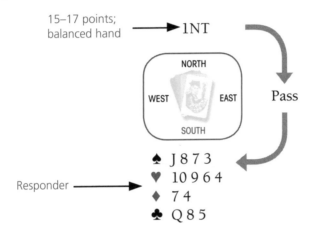

15–17 points; balanced hand ⟶ 1NT

Pass

Responder ⟶
♠ J 8 7 3
♥ 10 9 6 4
♦ 7 4
♣ Q 8 5

Pass. With only three high-card points, responder knows the partnership belongs in partscore. Responder would like to look for a major suit fit but would be awkwardly placed if opener were to reply 2♦ to a 2♣ inquiry. Responder would not want to pass and leave opener as declarer in a diamond contract. Responder would also not want to bid 2NT since that would be invitational, showing 8 or 9 points. So, responder's best choice is to pass and let opener play in 1NT.

There is one unusual exception. If responder is short in clubs, it is sometimes reasonable to use the Stayman convention with 0–7 points[15].

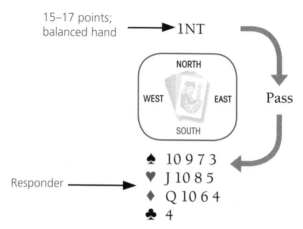

15–17 points;
balanced hand ⟶ 1NT

NORTH

WEST   EAST   Pass

SOUTH

♠ 10 9 7 3
Responder ⟶ ♥ J 10 8 5
♦ Q 10 6 4
♣ 4

2♣. Although responder has only 3 high-card points, there is little risk in using Stayman with this type of hand. If opener replies 2♥ or 2♠, responder can pass, leaving the partnership in partscore in an eight-card fit. If opener replies 2♦, responder can also pass, leaving opener to play a partscore in diamonds. This may not be a great spot if opener has only two or three diamonds but, with no four-card major, it is possible that opener has a four-card, or even a five-card, diamond suit.

---

[15] See Practice Deal # 29 for an example.

When Responder Has Clubs

When a conventional meaning is assigned to a bid, there is a cost: the natural meaning of the bid is lost. In the case of Stayman, for example, a response of 2♣ can no longer be used to show clubs. The reason Stayman is so popular, however, is that this loss is considered a small price to pay for the advantages associated with uncovering a major suit fit. However, the partnership still has to decide what to do when responder actually has clubs. In practical terms, the club suit can often be ignored when responding to 1NT. When the partnership belongs in partscore, responder can choose to play in notrump rather than clubs when holding a five-card or longer club suit; when the partnership belongs in game, responder usually places the contract in 3NT instead of looking to play in 5♣. For example:

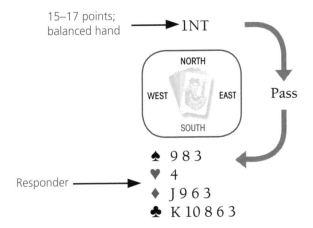

15–17 points; balanced hand ➞ 1NT

Pass

Responder ➞

♠ 9 8 3
♥ 4
♦ J 9 6 3
♣ K 10 8 6 3

Pass. Although 2♣ might be a better contract than 1NT, there's no guarantee and no practical method to find out if opener has three or more clubs without getting the partnership too high. So, responder simply passes and hopes for the best.

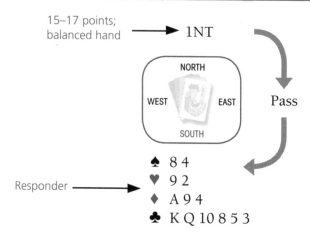

15–17 points; balanced hand ⟶ 1NT

Pass

NORTH

WEST   EAST

SOUTH

Responder ⟶

♠ 8 4
♥ 9 2
♦ A 9 4
♣ K Q 10 8 5 3

3NT. It's possible that 5♣ is a better contract but most of the time it will be easier to take nine tricks in 3NT than eleven tricks in 5♣. So, the practical approach is to ignore the club suit and raise to 3NT.

There are times, however, when responder does want to show a club suit. In Chapter 2 we'll see how responder, with a long club suit, can sign off in partscore or make an invitational bid.

When responder wants to make a forcing bid with a long club suit, the way to do it is to start with a bid of 2♣, which opener will assume is the Stayman convention, and then rebid 3♣. This shows a real club suit and is forcing[16].

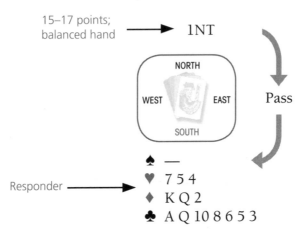

15–17 points; balanced hand ➝ 1NT

NORTH

WEST   EAST   Pass

SOUTH

Responder ➝

♠ —
♥ 7 5 4
♦ K Q 2
♣ A Q 10 8 6 5 3

2♣. Responder has enough strength to get the partnership to game, but with such an unbalanced hand, it's possible that 5♣ or even 6♣ might be a better contract than 3NT. To show the club suit, responder starts with 2♣. Opener will assume this is Stayman and will make an appropriate reply of 2♦, 2♥, or 2♠. Now responder shows a real club suit by rebidding 3♣. This is forcing and opener can choose to show support for clubs or bid 3NT with no interest in playing with clubs as the trump suit. The auction may be a little uncomfortable, but at least responder has introduced the possibility of playing in clubs.

---

[16] There are other agreements that can be used, but this is a fairly standard approach that integrates with the other methods introduced in this book.

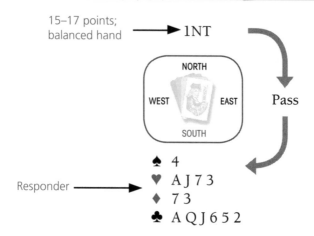

15–17 points; balanced hand ➤ 1NT

NORTH

WEST | EAST | Pass

SOUTH

Responder ➤

♠ 4
♥ A J 7 3
♦ 7 3
♣ A Q J 6 5 2

2♣. Here responder gets the best of both worlds. By starting with 2♣, responder can find out whether the partnership has an eight-card heart fit. If opener bids 2♥, responder can put the partnership in 4♥ or even consider slam (more about this in Chapter 4). If opener bids 2♦ or 2♠, responder can now bid 3♣ to show the club suit and investigate the possibility of playing in clubs rather than notrump.

Such hands for responder are rare, but it is still a good idea for the partnership to have an agreement about how to handle them.

When the Opponents Interfere

Modern players are very competitive. Even though the 1NT opening shows a fairly strong hand, the opponents will sometimes enter the auction. The situation is challenging because today's opponents often use artificial methods when interfering after a 1NT opening bid. That's a subject outside our current scope, but we still need to know how to find out if the 1NT opener has a four-card major when our right-hand opponent enters the auction. Here is a popular set of agreements[17]:

- If right-hand opponent *doubles*, a response of 2♣ is still the Stayman convention.
- If right-hand opponent overcalls 2♣, double is used to ask if opener has a four-card major.
- If right-hand opponent overcalls 2♦ or higher, a *cuebid* of the opponent's suit asks if opener has a four-card major.

For example:

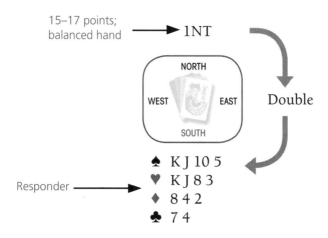

2♣. East's double doesn't take up any bidding room so it is reasonable to continue to use 2♣ as the Stayman convention.

---

[17] Many other agreements are possible, so it is a good idea to check with partner beforehand to make sure you are using the same methods.

If opener replies 2♥ or 2♠, responder can make an invitational raise to the three level. If opener bids 2♦, responder can make an invitational rebid of 2NT.

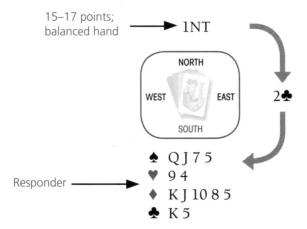

15–17 points; balanced hand → 1NT

2♣

Responder →

♠ Q J 7 5
♥ 9 4
♦ K J 10 8 5
♣ K 5

Double. When the overcall is 2♣, responder can use a double to take the place of the Stayman convention. If opener replies 2♠, responder can jump to 4♠. If opener replies 2♦ or 2♥, responder can put the partnership in 3NT.

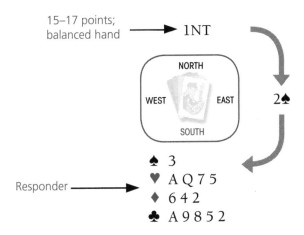

15–17 points; balanced hand ⟶ 1NT

NORTH
WEST EAST 2♠
SOUTH

♠ 3
♥ A Q 7 5
♦ 6 4 2
♣ A 9 8 5 2

Responder ⟶

3♠. When an opponent makes an overcall higher than **2♣**, the standard agreement is that a cuebid of the opponent's suit takes the place of the Stayman convention. A double of the overcall would be for *penalty*. On this hand, South can cuebid **3♠** to find out if opener has a four-card heart suit. Opener's options are to bid **4♥** with a four-card or longer heart suit and to bid 3NT otherwise. Responder must have enough strength—about 10 or more points—to use the cuebid since it will commit the partnership to at least the game level. If opener bids 3NT, responder will pass and hope that opener has some strength in spades.

If an opponent interferes after responder has used Stayman, opener can judge whether or not to show a four-card major suit[18].

WEST	NORTH	EAST	SOUTH
1NT	PASS	2♣	2♦
?			

♠ J 5 4
♥ A Q 6 3
♦ A 4
♣ K Q 7 5

2♥. South's 2♦ overcall doesn't prevent West from showing the four-card heart suit, the same bid West would have made if South had not interfered.

WEST	NORTH	EAST	SOUTH
1NT	PASS	2♣	2♠
?			

♠ J 5 4
♥ A Q 6 3
♦ A 4
♣ K Q 7 5

Pass. To show the hearts, West would have to bid 3♥. It is probably better to pass and leave further action to East. East might have spades and not hearts and might want to double South's overcall for penalty. If not, East will bid something else and West can show the heart suit at the next opportunity.

In Conclusion: Stayman is a useful way to get more information about WHERE to place the contract when partner makes an opening notrump bid or overcall.

---

[18] More complex agreements are possible, but this advice is practical.

SUMMARY

Opening 1NT

- 15–17 valuation points.
- A balanced hand.

The Stayman Convention

After a 1NT opening bid, Stayman, an artificial response of 2♣, is used to uncover an eight-card major suit fit.

Requirements for Stayman

- 8 or more points
- At least one four-card major suit

Opener's Reply to Stayman

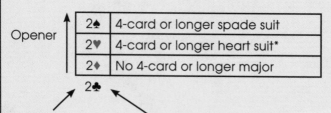

	2♠	4-card or longer spade suit
Opener	2♥	4-card or longer heart suit*
	2♦	No 4-card or longer major

2♣

Responder   Stayman

* With four hearts and four spades, opener bids 2♥ in response to Stayman, bidding "*up the line.*"

Responder's Rebid After Using Stayman

After hearing opener's reply, responder can usually decide How High and Where. If not, responder can make a further invitational bid with 8–9 points (e.g. 2NT or a raise to 3♥ or 3♠) or a forcing bid with 10 or more points (e.g. a *new suit* at the three level).

Other Considerations for Stayman

AFTER A 1NT OVERCALL
Stayman can be used by advancer to uncover an eight-card major suit fit.

STAYMAN WITH 0–7 POINTS
Stayman is used only if responder is short in clubs.

WHEN RESPONDER HAS CLUBS
Chapter 2 discusses how responder, with a long club suit, can sign off in partscore or make an invitational bid. With 10 or more points, responder uses Stayman and then bids clubs.

WHEN THE OPPONENTS INTERFERE
Here are popular agreements after responder's right-hand opponent interferes:

Right-hand Opponent's Action	Responder's Action
Double	A response of 2♣ is still Stayman
Overcall 2♣	Double is used as Stayman
Overcall of 2♦ or higher	A cuebid of the opponent's suit is used as Stayman

Quiz – Part I

South is the dealer. What *call* would South make with the following hands?

WEST	NORTH	EAST	SOUTH
			?

a) ♠ 8 7 3
♥ K J 7
♦ A Q J
♣ K Q 7 3

b) ♠ K Q 7 5
♥ A J 8 4
♦ K 2
♣ Q 7 2

c) ♠ A J
♥ K 8 2
♦ A J 10 7 4
♣ Q J 5

d) ♠ J 8 7 4
♥ K 9
♦ K Q 8 3
♣ A 9 2

e) ♠ A Q 7
♥ K J 10 5
♦ A K 5
♣ Q 9 3

f) ♠ A J 5
♥ K J 7 6 3
♦ 8 6
♣ K Q J

North opens 1NT. East passes. As responder, what call would South make with the following hands?

WEST	NORTH	EAST	SOUTH
	1NT	PASS	?

g) ♠ Q 10 8 3
♥ K 9 7 5
♦ A Q
♣ 7 5 2

h) ♠ 9 3
♥ A Q 10 6
♦ K 10 9 8 2
♣ 6 2

i) ♠ 5 2
♥ 9 7
♦ Q 9 7 4
♣ A K J 9 8

j) ♠ 9 4
♥ Q J 6 3
♦ A J 10 7
♣ 8 6 4

k) ♠ 10 8 7 3
♥ J 9 6 4
♦ 8 5
♣ J 8 7

l) ♠ J 8 6 3
♥ Q 7 5 4
♦ Q 8 6 3 2
♣ —

Answers to Quiz – Part I

a)   **1NT.** A balanced hand with 4-3-3-3 distribution and 16 high-card points.

b)   **1NT.** This hand has 15 high-card points and a balanced *pattern*, 4-4-3-2.

c)   **1NT.** A 5-3-3-2 pattern is balanced and this hand has 16 high-card points plus 1 length point for the five-card diamond suit, putting it in the range for 1NT.

d)   **1♦.** The hand is balanced but has only 13 high-card points, not enough to open 1NT. With no five-card major suit, the longer minor suit is opened.

e)   **1♣.** This is a balanced hand with 19 high-card points, too much to open 1NT. With no five-card major and three cards in both minor suits, it's standard practice to open 1♣.

f)   **1NT.** With 5-3-3-2 distribution, this is a balanced hand. With 15 high-card points plus 1 length point for the five-card heart suit, the hand falls into the range for a 1NT opening. This takes priority over opening in the major suit, even with a low doubleton in diamonds.

g)   **2♣.** With 11 high-card points, South knows How High—game—since the partnership has at least 26 combined points. To answer Where, South uses Stayman, 2♣, to discover whether North holds a four-card major suit.

h)   **2♣.** With 9 high-card points plus 1 length point, South uses Stayman to find out whether North has a four-card heart suit. That will determine whether the partnership belongs in 3NT or 4♥.

i)   **3NT.** South has enough strength to take the partnership to game. With no interest in looking for a major suit fit, South settles for 3NT. Even if the partnership has an eight-card or longer minor suit fit, it should be easier to take nine tricks in notrump that eleven tricks in 5♣ or 5♦.

j)   **2♣.** With 8 high-card points South isn't sure How High or Where the partnership belongs. South starts with Stayman to determine whether the partnership has an eight-card heart fit. After getting the answer to this question, South will invite opener to bid game with a maximum.

k)   **Pass.** Although the partnership might have an eight-card fit in hearts or spades, South doesn't have enough strength to use Stayman without the risk of getting the partnership too high. South settles for 1NT.

l)   **2♣.** Although South has only 5 high-card points and 1 length point, it is safe to use Stayman when short in clubs. South plans to pass whatever rebid North makes: 2♦, 2♥, or 2♠.

Quiz – Part II

South opens 1NT, West passes, and North responds 2♣, the Stayman convention. After East passes, what rebid would South make with each of the following hands?

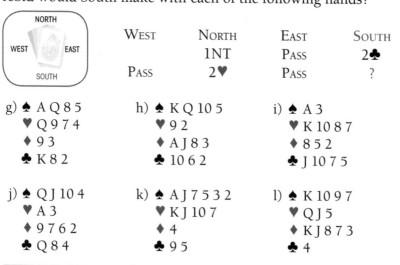

	WEST	NORTH	EAST	SOUTH
				1NT
	PASS	2♣	PASS	?

a) ♠ A K 5
♥ K Q 4
♦ 10 3
♣ Q J 9 6 2

b) ♠ Q 7
♥ K J 8 4
♦ A Q 8 5
♣ A J 3

c) ♠ 9 7 6 2
♥ A K J
♦ Q 10 7 5
♣ A J

d) ♠ A Q 10 5
♥ K 9 7 3
♦ A 10
♣ K J 4

e) ♠ K 10 8 7 5
♥ A Q 6
♦ Q 9 5
♣ A 6

f) ♠ J 4
♥ A K Q
♦ J 9 6 2
♣ A Q 7 3

North opens 1NT, South responds 2♣ and North rebids 2♥. What rebid would South make with each of the following hands?

	WEST	NORTH	EAST	SOUTH
		1NT	PASS	2♣
	PASS	2♥	PASS	?

g) ♠ A Q 8 5
♥ Q 9 7 4
♦ 9 3
♣ K 8 2

h) ♠ K Q 10 5
♥ 9 2
♦ A J 8 3
♣ 10 6 2

i) ♠ A 3
♥ K 10 8 7
♦ 8 5 2
♣ J 10 7 5

j) ♠ Q J 10 4
♥ A 3
♦ 9 7 6 2
♣ Q 8 4

k) ♠ A J 7 5 3 2
♥ K J 10 7
♦ 4
♣ 9 5

l) ♠ K 10 9 7
♥ Q J 5
♦ K J 8 7 3
♣ 4

Answers to Quiz – Part II

a) 2♦. With no four-card major, South rebids 2♦. The 2♦ call is artificial and says nothing about South's diamond suit.

b) 2♥. With a four-card heart suit, South responds 2♥ to the Stayman inquiry.

c) 2♠. South rebids 2♠ to show the four-card spade suit. The quality of the spades is of no concern, only that South has four of them.

d) 2♥. With four cards in both major suits, standard practice is to bid 'up the line', showing the hearts first.

e) 2♠. A 2♠ rebid by the 1NT opener shows a four-card or longer spade suit.

f) 2♦. With no four-card major, opener replies 2♦ to the Stayman convention.

g) 4♥. Having found an eight-card fit in hearts, South has the answer to both How High, game, and Where, hearts.

h) 3NT. South knows How High, game, and was looking for an eight-card fit in spades. When North bids hearts, South puts the partnership in game in notrump. If North also has four spades, North will now bid 4♠, inferring that South must have been looking for a fit in that suit.

i) 3♥. By using Stayman, South has found Where the partnership belongs, hearts. With 8 high-card points, South now makes an invitational raise to 3♥ to find out How High the partnership belongs–partscore or game.

j) 2NT. With 9 high-card points, South makes an invitational bid of 2NT after searching for a spade fit by using the Stayman convention.

k) 4♥. With at least one four-card major, South starts with Stayman. After finding a fit, South takes the partnership to game.

l) 3NT. South was looking for an eight-card spade fit but hasn't found one. South's next responsibility is to show there is enough combined strength for game. South doesn't worry about the singleton club. 3NT should be the best game contract.

Quiz – Part III

North opens 1NT, South responds 2♣ and North rebids 2♦. What rebid would South make with each of the following hands?

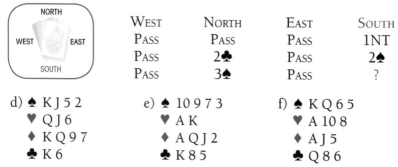

WEST	NORTH	EAST	SOUTH
PASS	1NT	PASS	2♣
PASS	2♦	PASS	?

a) ♠ K J 8 6
♥ A Q 9 5
♦ Q 8 5 2
♣ 3

b) ♠ Q 10 7 4
♥ A 2
♦ Q 9 8 7 2
♣ 7 4

c) ♠ K J 9 7 2
♥ A Q 8 4
♦ 9 8 3
♣ 4

South opens 1NT, North responds 2♣, and South bids 2♠. North now raises to 3♠. What call would South make with these hands?

WEST	NORTH	EAST	SOUTH
PASS	PASS	PASS	1NT
PASS	2♣	PASS	2♠
PASS	3♠	PASS	?

d) ♠ K J 5 2
♥ Q J 6
♦ K Q 9 7
♣ K 6

e) ♠ 10 9 7 3
♥ A K
♦ A Q J 2
♣ K 8 5

f) ♠ K Q 6 5
♥ A 10 8
♦ A J 5
♣ Q 8 6

South opens 1NT, North responds 2♣, and South bids 2♥. North now bids 3NT. What call would South make with these hands?

WEST	NORTH	EAST	SOUTH
			1NT
PASS	2♣	PASS	2♥
PASS	3NT	PASS	?

g) ♠ 8 4
♥ A K J 7
♦ A Q 8 3
♣ Q 9 2

h) ♠ K 10 4
♥ K Q 8 7 3
♦ A J
♣ Q 9 5

i) ♠ Q 7 5 2
♥ A K 8 4
♦ J 5
♣ A Q J

Answers to Quiz – Part III

a) **3NT**. Stayman has revealed there is no eight-card major suit fit but South has 12 high-card points, enough to go to game. Nine tricks in notrump should be easier than anything else, even though South has a singleton.

b) **2NT**. After looking for a fit in spades, South rebids 2NT to show an invitational hand of about 8–9 points.

c) **3♠**. North doesn't have a four-card major suit but there may still be an eight-card fit in spades. With enough to go to game, South makes a forcing jump to 3♠, asking opener to bid either 3NT with a doubleton spade or 4♠ with three-card support for spades.

d) **Pass**. North is inviting opener to bid game. With only 15 high-card points, a minimum for the opening bid of 1NT, South declines the invitation and settles for partscore.

e) **4♠**. With 17 high-card points, South has a maximum for the opening bid of 1NT and should accept the invitation. South doesn't worry about the quality of the spade suit; the partnership has an eight-card fit.

f) **Pass/4♠**. This is a borderline decision, with 16 high-card points. Passing is the conservative action; accepting the invitation is the aggressive action. Either choice could work out well.

g) **Pass**. North used the Stayman convention and then chose 3NT after hearing about South's four-card heart suit. Presumably, North was interested in finding a spade fit, not a heart fit. 3NT should be the best spot for the partnership.

h) **Pass**. The 2♥ reply to the Stayman convention showed a four-card **or longer** heart suit. North has shown no interest in hearts and may have only one or two. Accept North's decision to play game in 3NT.

i) **4♠**. North used Stayman but wasn't interested in playing in hearts when South showed a four-card suit. Presumably, North was looking for a fit in spades and is now showing enough strength to play in game. South should put the partnership in its 'known' eight-card spade fit.

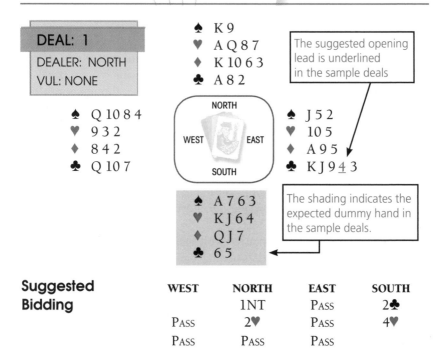

DEAL: 1

DEALER: NORTH

VUL: NONE

NORTH
♠ K 9
♥ A Q 8 7
♦ K 10 6 3
♣ A 8 2

The suggested opening lead is underlined in the sample deals

WEST
♠ Q 10 8 4
♥ 9 3 2
♦ 8 4 2
♣ Q 10 7

EAST
♠ J 5 2
♥ 10 5
♦ A 9 5
♣ K J 9 4 3

SOUTH
♠ A 7 6 3
♥ K J 6 4
♦ Q J 7
♣ 6 5

The shading indicates the expected dummy hand in the sample deals.

Suggested Bidding

WEST	NORTH	EAST	SOUTH
	1NT	PASS	2♣
PASS	2♥	PASS	4♥
PASS	PASS	PASS	

With a balanced hand and 16 high-card points, North opens 1NT. East passes.

With 11 high-card points, South has the answer to How High, game. The only question is Where: 3NT, 4♥ or 4♠? To discover whether the partnership has an eight-card fit in a major suit, South uses the Stayman convention. The artificial 2♣ response asks whether opener has a four-card or longer major suit. With a four-card heart suit, North bids 2♥.

South now knows Where as well as How High and puts the partnership in the major suit game, 4♥.

Suggested Opening Lead

With no *sequence* to lead from, East might choose to lead from the long suit, clubs, hoping to develop tricks through *promotion* and length. East would lead the fourth highest, the ♣4.

Declarer's Plan[19]

Declarer starts by <u>A</u>ssessing the situation. North's goal is to take 10 tricks. There are two spade winners, four hearts, and the ♣A.

So, North moves to the second planning stage and <u>B</u>rowses Declarer's Checklist. North can plan to promote three winners in the diamond suit. North can also plan to trump a club in the dummy. There are more than enough

---

DECLARER'S PLAN—THE ABC'S

Declarer: North   Contract: 4♥

A SSESS THE SITUATION

Goal	10
Sure Tricks	7
Extra Tricks Needed	3

B ROWSE DECLARER'S CHECKLIST

Promotion	3 in diamonds
Length	
The Finesse	
Trumping in Dummy	1 in clubs

C ONSIDER THE ORDER

• Draw trumps.

---

tricks so, when <u>C</u>onsidering the Order, declarer's priority is to *draw trumps*. After winning the ♣A, declarer plays three rounds of trumps to remove all the opponents' trumps when they are divided 3-2. Then declarer can lead diamonds, starting with the ♦Q or ♦J, high card from the short side. Once the defenders take their ♦A, declarer has three diamond winners.

The defenders can take a club winner, but that's all. Declarer can trump a third round of clubs with dummy's last heart and make an *overtrick*. The only tricks lost are the ♦A and a club.

Comments

North-South do well to play with hearts as the trump suit and can take eleven tricks. If North-South did not use the Stayman convention and reached 3NT, they would be defeated if East led the ♣4, fourth highest. After the ♣A is driven out, declarer only has four hearts and two spades as *sure tricks*. To promote enough tricks to make 3NT, declarer will have to lead diamonds. East can win the ♦A and take enough club winners to defeat 3NT. East-West get the ♦A and four club tricks. So, there is a three trick difference on this deal between playing in notrump and playing in the 4-4 heart fit.

---

[19] See Appendix 1 for a description of the ABC's of Declarer's Play.

	DEAL: 2	♠ 8 5 2
	DEALER: EAST	♥ A 10
	VUL: N-S	♦ Q J 10 8 3
		♣ 9 5 4

WEST
♠ A Q J
♥ 7 3 2
♦ K 6 5
♣ K Q J 8

NORTH

WEST   EAST

SOUTH

EAST
♠ 9 6 3
♥ Q 9 5 4
♦ A 7
♣ A 7 6 3

SOUTH
♠ K 10 7 4
♥ K J 8 6
♦ 9 4 2
♣ 10 2

Suggested Bidding

WEST	NORTH	EAST	SOUTH
		PASS	PASS
1NT	PASS	2♣	PASS
2♦	PASS	3NT	PASS
PASS	PASS		

East and South pass. West opens 1NT with a balanced hand and 16 high-card points. North passes.

With 10 high-card points, East knows How High the partnership belongs, game. East isn't sure whether the partnership belongs in 3NT or 4♥. To look for an eight-card heart fit, East responds 2♣, the Stayman convention. South passes.

With no four-card or longer major suit, West makes the artificial response of 2♦. This says nothing about diamonds.

Since there is no eight-card or longer major suit fit, East puts the partnership in the most likely game contract, 3NT.

Suggested Opening Lead

North leads the ♦Q, top of the solid sequence.

Declarer's Plan

After North makes the opening lead and the East hand comes down as the dummy, West makes a plan. As declarer, West's goal is to take at least nine tricks to make the 3NT contract. West begins by counting the sure winners: one spade, two diamonds, and four clubs for a total of seven tricks. Two more tricks are required.

Moving to the second stage,

West browses Declarer's Checklist. The spade suit could provide an extra trick through promotion by simply driving out the ♠K, but a better plan is to try to get two extra tricks from the spade suit with the help of a *repeated finesse*[20]. To do this, declarer must make use of the two *entries* to the dummy, the ♦A and ♣A.

After winning a trick with the ♦A[21], declarer leads a spade and finesses the ♠J, hoping South holds the ♠K. When this succeeds, declarer can get back to dummy with the ♣A and lead another spade and finesse the ♠Q. The repeated finesse works and declarer gets three tricks from the spade suit without losing a trick to the defenders. Together with the two diamond tricks and four club tricks, declarer has the nine tricks needed to make 3NT.

Comments

After using Stayman, East puts the partnership in 3NT when an eight-card major suit fit can't be found. Although the partnership has an eight-card fit in clubs, it will usually be easier to take nine tricks in notrump than eleven tricks in a minor suit. On this deal, in a contract of 5♣ East-West would lose three heart tricks.

---

[20] See Appendix 1 for a description of the repeated finesse.

[21] Declarer could win the first trick with the ♦K and use the ♣A as the first entry to take a spade finesse. The ♦A could then be used later to repeat the spade finesse.

DEAL: 3

DEALER: SOUTH
VUL: E-W

North:
♠ Q 10 8 4
♥ A 7 6 3
♦ 9 4
♣ Q 6 2

West:
♠ 7 3
♥ J 10 8 4
♦ A J 8 5 2
♣ 9 4

East:
♠ A 6 2
♥ Q 9 2
♦ K 10 7
♣ 10 8 7 3

South:
♠ K J 9 5
♥ K 5
♦ Q 6 3
♣ A K J 5

Suggested Bidding

WEST	NORTH	EAST	SOUTH
			1NT
Pass	2♣	Pass	2♠
Pass	3♠	Pass	4♠
Pass	Pass	Pass	

South opens 1NT with 17 high-card points and a balanced hand. West passes.

North has 8 high-card points, so North isn't sure about How High. There may be enough combined strength for game if South has a maximum of 17 points. Otherwise, the partnership should stop in partscore. So, North wants to invite South to game. North also isn't sure Where. The partnership could have an eight-card major suit fit; otherwise the partnership should play in notrump. To handle both challenges, North starts with 2♣, the Stayman convention.

South has a four-card spade suit and bids 2♠ in reply to Stayman. Now North knows Where the partnership belongs. To invite opener to game, North raises to 3♠. With a maximum for the 1NT opening, South accepts the invitation and continues to 4♠, resolving the challenge of How High.

Suggested Opening Lead

Against a suit contract West doesn't want to lead away from an ace. West might choose the ♥J, top of the broken sequence in hearts.

Declarer's Plan

South's goal is to take at least ten tricks. South can count on two sure trick in hearts and four in clubs. That's a total of six tricks, four short of the goal.

South browses Declarer's Checklist for ways to develop the extra tricks. Three tricks can be promoted in the spade suit. A fourth trick can be developed by giving up two diamond tricks and then *trumping* a diamond in dummy.

```
┌─ DECLARER'S PLAN—THE ABC'S ─┐

Declarer: South    Contract: 4♠

ASSESS THE SITUATION
Goal                  10
Sure Tricks            6
Extra Tricks Needed    4

BROWSE DECLARER'S CHECKLIST
Promotion          3 in spades
Length
The Finesse
Trumping in Dummy  1 in diamonds

CONSIDER THE ORDER
 • Draw trumpos.
 • Leave a spade in the dummy to
   trump a diamond.
```

Since only one spade needs to be left in dummy, after winning the first heart trick South can start by drawing trumps. South leads spades, driving out the defender's ♠A. The defenders can take two diamond tricks, but that's all. Declarer's last diamond is trumped with dummy's last spade.

Comments

North-South do well to reach 4♠. If North-South were in 3NT, East-West could defeat the contract. West would start with the ♦5, fourth highest from longest and strongest. East can win the first trick with the ♦K and lead back the ♦10, trapping declarer's ♦Q. The defenders take the first five diamond tricks.

	♠ J 2
DEAL: 4	♥ A Q 9 4
DEALER: WEST	♦ Q 10 9 3 2
VUL: BOTH	♣ 10 4

```
                     NORTH
   ♠  A 6 5 4                        ♠  K 8
   ♥  10 7 5 2    WEST  ⟨ ⟩ EAST     ♥  J 6 3
   ♦  K 6 4                          ♦  A 8 5
   ♣  Q 3                            ♣  A K 8 6 2
                     SOUTH
```

♠ Q 10 9 7 3
♥ K 8
♦ J 7
♣ J 9 7 5

Suggested Bidding

WEST	NORTH	EAST	SOUTH
PASS	PASS	1NT	PASS
2♣	PASS	2♦	PASS
2NT	PASS	PASS	PASS

After two passes, East opens 1NT with 15 high-card points plus 1 point for a five-card suit. South doesn't have enough strength to overcall at the two level and passes.

West, with 9 high-card points, has enough to invite the partnership to game. West would also like to find an eight-card major suit fit if the partnership has one. So, West starts with the Stayman convention by responding 2♣.

With no four-card or longer major, East makes the artificial response of 2♦. This has nothing to do with diamonds.

West now knows the partnership doesn't have an eight-card major suit fit. West invites East to bid game by rebidding 2NT. This is similar to raising 1NT to 2NT, but West checked first for a major.

With a near minimum—15 high-card points plus 1 for the five-card suit—East declines the invitation and passes[22].

---

[22] With 16 points—15 high-card points plus 1 for the five-card suit—East is on the borderline for accepting. East could bid 3NT, which would make if the missing clubs were divided 3-3 instead of 4-2. Slightly against the odds, but a reasonable contract.

Suggested Opening Lead

South makes the opening lead. South would lead the ♠10, top of the interior sequence in that suit.

Declarer's Plan

East is declarer and the goal is to take eight tricks. East counts two sure tricks in spades, two in diamonds, and three in clubs. One more trick needs to be developed.

Browsing Declarer's Checklist, there is an opportunity to get one or more extra tricks through length in clubs. There is also the possibility of getting an extra trick in hearts if they divide 3-3, but the club suit offers a much better chance.

```
┌─ DECLARER'S PLAN—THE ABC'S ─┐
  Declarer: East    Contract: 2NT

  ASSESS THE SITUATION
   Goal                   8
   Sure Tricks            7
   Extra Tricks Needed    1

  BROWSE DECLARER'S CHECKLIST
   Promotion
   Length              1 or 2 in clubs
                       1 in hearts
   The Finesse

  CONSIDER THE ORDER
   • Take the losses early in clubs.
   • High card from short side first.
```

After winning the first spade trick, declarer should start developing the club suit right away. Declarer starts by playing dummy's ♣Q, high card from the short side first. Then declarer takes the ♣A and ♣K. If the missing clubs were divided 3-3, declarer's two remaining clubs would be winners. When North *discards* on the third round of clubs, declarer knows the missing clubs are divided 4-2. That's okay. Declarer can play a fourth round of clubs, giving up a trick to the opponents. That establishes declarer's remaining club as a winner, the eighth trick needed to make the contract.

Comments

East-West do well to stop in partscore on this deal. When the clubs don't divide exactly 3-3, eight tricks are all that are available.

Conceal your dispositions, and your condition will remain secret, which leads to victory; show your dispositions, and your condition will become patent, which leads to defeat.

—Sun Tzu, The Art of War

Jacoby Transfer Bids

Jacoby transfer bids are used by responder after a notrump opening bid. The most frequent explanation of why transfer bids have become so popular is that by responding in an artificial manner, the weaker hand will become the dummy and the stronger hand, the 1NT opener, will remain hidden. To see the advantage of this, consider the following deal where North opens 1NT and South takes the partnership to game in hearts:

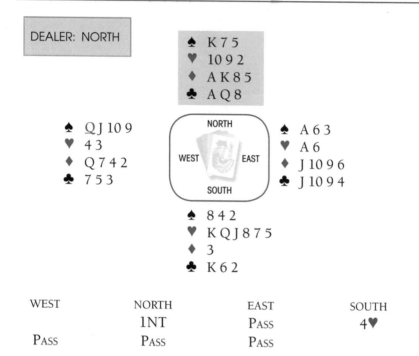

WEST	NORTH	EAST	SOUTH
	1NT	PASS	4♥
PASS	PASS	PASS	

West is on lead and will likely lead the ♠Q, top of the sequence. This is right through North's strength. It allows the defenders to trap the ♠K and take the first three spade tricks. They will later get the ♥A to defeat the contract.

Now let's suppose we turn the deal upside down and make the 1NT opener the declarer in the 4♥ contract:

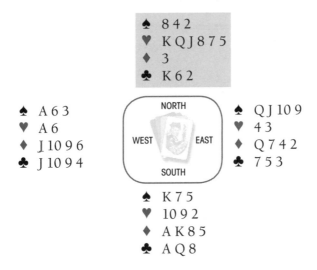

```
                    ♠ 8 4 2
                    ♥ K Q J 8 7 5
                    ♦ 3
                    ♣ K 6 2

   ♠ A 6 3           NORTH            ♠ Q J 10 9
   ♥ A 6                              ♥ 4 3
   ♦ J 10 9 6    WEST       EAST      ♦ Q 7 4 2
   ♣ J 10 9 4                         ♣ 7 5 3
                    SOUTH

                    ♠ K 7 5
                    ♥ 10 9 2
                    ♦ A K 8 5
                    ♣ A Q 8
```

Now the lead is up to the stronger hand, the 1NT opener. The contract can no longer be defeated because South's ♠K can't be trapped. If the ♠A is led, South will get a trick with the ♠K. If another suit is led, declarer can take ten tricks after playing the ♦A-K, discarding a spade from dummy, and then driving out the ♥A. Declarer gets five heart tricks, two diamonds, and three clubs.

Making the weaker hand the dummy was originally only an idea. There had to be a bidding system to make this happen. The notrump opener had to bid the suit first, hearts in the above example, to become the declarer. Oswald Jacoby popularized ideas developed by David Carter of the United States and Olle Willner of Sweden to bring this about.

The Jacoby Transfer Bid

The mechanics for Jacoby transfers are:

Using Jacoby Transfer Responses to 1NT

- With 5 or more spades, responder bids 2♥.
- With 5 or more hearts, responder bids 2♦.

Responder doesn't need any high-card points to make a transfer response, only a five-card or longer major suit.

When responder makes a transfer bid, the 1NT opener rebids as follows.

1NT Opener's Rebid After a Transfer

- Bid 2♠ if responder bids 2♥.
- Bid 2♥ if responder bids 2♦.

Examples of Opener's Rebid After a Jacoby Transfer Bid

After opening 1NT and hearing a 2♦ or 2♥ transfer response, opener's rebid is automatic[23]. Here are examples after opener bids 1NT and responder bids 2♦.

OPENER	RESPONDER	
1NT	2♦ ←	Jacoby transfer showing 5 or more hearts.
?		

♠ K J 8
♥ A 9 3
♦ K Q 10 8 5
♣ Q 10

2♥. Responder's 2♦ bid is totally artificial, having nothing to do with diamonds. Opener simply accepts the transfer by bidding hearts, the requested suit.

---

[23] With four-card support for responder's major and a maximum, opener can *super-accept* the transfer by jumping to the three level, but that's outside the scope of this book.

♠ A Q J 8
♥ 7 4
♦ K 10 7
♣ A K 6 3

2♥. The 2♦ transfer bid doesn't ask whether opener likes hearts. It's a command for opener to bid 2♥, even with a low doubleton.

Here is an example after responder bids 2♥ as a transfer to spades.

OPENER	RESPONDER	
1NT	2♥ ◄	Jacoby transfer showing 5 or more spades.
?		

♠ Q 7
♥ A K J 5
♦ J 7 5 2
♣ K Q 4

2♠. Opener accepts the transfer. Opener can't pass the 2♥ transfer since responder may have no hearts and may also be planning to bid again[24].

---

[24] Opener can only pass the transfer bid if opener's right-hand opponent bids or doubles.

Using the Jacoby Transfer

Let's see how the use of transfers would work with our earlier deal.

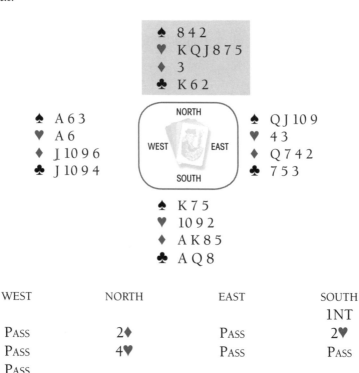

```
              ♠ 8 4 2
              ♥ K Q J 8 7 5
              ♦ 3
              ♣ K 6 2

♠ A 6 3          NORTH          ♠ Q J 10 9
♥ A 6                           ♥ 4 3
♦ J 10 9 6   WEST      EAST     ♦ Q 7 4 2
♣ J 10 9 4                      ♣ 7 5 3
                 SOUTH
              ♠ K 7 5
              ♥ 10 9 2
              ♦ A K 8 5
              ♣ A Q 8
```

WEST	NORTH	EAST	SOUTH
			1NT
Pass	2♦	Pass	2♥
Pass	4♥	Pass	Pass
Pass			

South opens 1NT and North uses the Jacoby transfer response of 2♦, asking opener to bid 2♥. South duly accepts the transfer by bidding 2♥ and North, knowing the partnership has enough strength and enough hearts to go for the game bonus, raises to 4♥. The partnership reaches game, but South becomes the declarer in hearts since South bid the suit first. North's artificial 2♦ transfer bid has accomplished the objective of making South, the stronger hand, the declarer. With West on lead, the 4♥ contract cannot be defeated.

Transfer bids require that both players understand how to make the best use of the convention. The key is that use of Jacoby transfers allows the partnership to:

- Get to the best game contract when responder knows there is enough combined strength to go for the game bonus;
- Invite game when the partnership may have enough combined strength;
- Stop in partscore when there is not enough combined strength for game.

Using Transfers When Responder Has a Strong Hand of 10–15 Points

With 10–15 points[25], responder has the answer to How High, game. The only question is Where?

WHEN RESPONDER HAS A SIX-CARD OR LONGER MAJOR SUIT

With a six-card or longer major suit, responder knows Where. Opener has at least two cards in the major suit, so the partnership has an eight-card fit. Responder transfers to the major suit and then takes the partnership to game in the major. Here are some examples for responder after partner opens 1NT.

---

[25] With 16 or more points, responder is interested in investigating a slam contract. Slam bidding is discussed in Chapter 4.

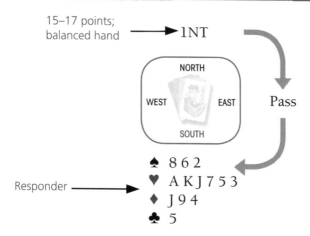

15–17 points; balanced hand ⟶ 1NT

NORTH

WEST   EAST   Pass

SOUTH

♠ 8 6 2
Responder ⟶ ♥ A K J 7 5 3
♦ J 9 4
♣ 5

2♦. With 9 high-card points plus 2 length points for the six-card suit, responder knows the partnership has at least 26 combined points (15 + 11), enough for game. With six hearts, responder also knows the partnership has at least an eight-card heart fit. So, responder can decide that the best contract for the partnership is 4♥. Using standard methods, responder would simply bid 4♥. Using transfers, responder starts by bidding 2♦ to get opener to bid 2♥. Then responder jumps to 4♥. The 4♥ contract is played by the 1NT opener, keeping the stronger hand concealed.

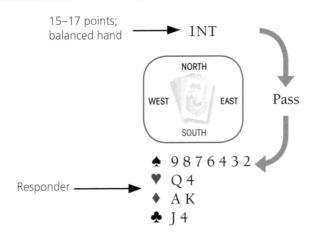

15–17 points; balanced hand ⟶ 1NT

NORTH

WEST ⬥ EAST   Pass

SOUTH

♠ 9 8 7 6 4 3 2
Responder ⟶ ♥ Q 4
♦ A K
♣ J 4

2♥. With 10 high-card points plus 3 length points for the seven-card spade suit, responder knows the partnership has at least 28 combined points (15 + 13). With seven spades, responder also knows the partnership has at least a nine-card spade fit. So, responder wants the partnership to play at the game level in spades. Using transfers, responder starts with 2♥ to tell opener to bid 2♠. Then responder raises to 4♠, putting the partnership where it belongs. Notice that responder doesn't need high-card strength in the major suit. The key is that the partnership has at least an eight-card or longer-suit fit and enough combined strength for game.

WHEN RESPONDER HAS A FIVE-CARD MAJOR SUIT

With only a five-card major suit, responder cannot be sure that there is an eight-card major suit fit. Opener might have only two cards in the major. So, responder transfers to the major suit and then jumps to 3NT to offer opener a choice of contracts. With a doubleton in responder's major, opener passes and the partnership will play game in notrump. With three-card or longer support for the major suit shown by responder, opener puts the partnership in game in the major.

For example, suppose these are the combined partnership hands:

Opener	Responder
♠ A Q J 3	♠ K 4
♥ 7 4	♥ A 10 8 5 3
♦ K Q 6	♦ J 3
♣ A 9 6 3	♣ K J 7 2

The auction would proceed:

Opener	Responder
1NT	2♦
2♥	3NT
Pass	

Opener bids 1NT with a balanced hand and 16 high-card points. With a five-card heart suit, responder starts with a Jacoby transfer bid of 2♦. Opener bids 2♥, as requested. Having already shown the heart suit through the transfer, and knowing the partnership has enough combined strength for game, responder now jumps to 3NT, offering a choice of games. With only a doubleton heart, opener passes responder's 3NT and the partnership plays the game contract in notrump.

3NT is the best contract. Declarer has four sure tricks in spades, one in hearts, and two in clubs. Two more tricks can be promoted in diamonds. A 4♥ contract might be defeated. The defenders will get the ♦A and perhaps three heart tricks, or more if the six missing hearts are divided 4-2 or worse.

Now let's change opener's hand:

OPENER	RESPONDER
♠ A Q J 3	♠ K 4
♥ K Q 6	♥ A 10 8 5 3
♦ 7 4	♦ J 3
♣ A 9 6 3	♣ K J 7 2

OPENER	RESPONDER
1NT	2♦
2♥	3NT
4♥	PASS

The auction begins the same way, but with three-card support for hearts, opener chooses to play game in 4♥ rather than 3NT. 4♥ is the best contract. 3NT is likely to be defeated if the opponents lead diamonds.

Using Transfers When Responder Has an Invitational Hand of 8–9 Points

With 8 or 9 points, responder is unsure How High the partnership belongs. If opener has a maximum, 17 points, the partnership has 25 (17 + 8) or 26 (17 + 9) points, enough to go for the game bonus. If not, the partnership likely belongs in a partscore contract.

WHEN RESPONDER HAS A SIX-CARD OR LONGER MAJOR SUIT

With a six-card or longer major suit, responder knows Where. Opener has at least two cards in the major suit, so the partnership has an eight-card fit. Responder transfers to the major suit and then invites opener to game by raising the suit to the three level. Opener can now continue to game in the major with a maximum, or pass and settle for partscore with a minimum[26]. Here are some examples for responder after partner opens 1NT.

---

[26] 16 points is a borderline decision for opener. Opener can choose whether to be conservative and pass or to be aggressive and accept the invitation.

For example, suppose these are the combined partnership hands:

	OPENER		RESPONDER
♠	A 7 4 3	♠	8 2
♥	J 9	♥	Q 10 7 6 4 2
♦	K Q 4	♦	A 7 5
♣	K Q 10 5	♣	J 8

The auction would proceed:

OPENER	RESPONDER
1NT	2♦
2♥	3♥
PASS	

Opener bids 1NT with a balanced hand and 15 high-card points. With a six-card heart suit, responder starts with a Jacoby transfer bid of 2♦. Opener bids 2♥, as requested, even with a doubleton heart. With 9 points, responder now invites opener to game by raising to 3♥. With a minimum, opener rejects the invitation by passing. The partnership stops in a partscore contract of 3♥.

3♥ is high enough for the partnership. The defenders will likely get a spade trick along with the ♥A–K and ♣A. 3NT is unlikely to make since the defenders could establish three or more spade tricks to go with the ♥A–K and ♣A.

Now let's change opener's hand:

OPENER	RESPONDER
♠ A 7 4 3	♠ 8 2
♥ J 9	♥ Q 10 7 6 4 2
♦ K Q 4	♦ A 7 5
♣ A K 10 5	♣ J 8

OPENER	RESPONDER
1NT	2♦
2♥	3♥
4♥	PASS

The auction begins the same way, but with a maximum, opener accepts the invitation and continues to game in 4♥, which is likely to make. Declarer can promote four winners in hearts to go with the ♠A, ♦A–K–Q, and ♣A–K for ten tricks.

WHEN RESPONDER HAS A FIVE-CARD MAJOR SUIT

With 8 or 9 points and a five-card major, responder has two challenges. Responder is unsure HOW HIGH the partnership belongs and also WHERE, since responder can't be sure there is an eight-card major suit fit. To resolve both issues, responder transfers to the major suit and then bids 2NT. By transferring and then bidding notrump, responder lets opener know about the five-card major suit and gives opener a choice of playing in notrump or the major. Opener can choose notrump with only two cards in the major and can choose to play in the major with three-card or longer support. That solves the problem of WHERE. By rebidding only 2NT, responder shows invitational strength. Opener can stop in partscore with a minimum or continue to game with a maximum. That solves the question of HOW HIGH.

For example, suppose these are the combined partnership hands:

OPENER	RESPONDER
♠ 5 4	♠ A 10 9 6 3
♥ A K J 3	♥ Q 4
♦ Q 10 9 5	♦ 7 3
♣ K Q 7	♣ J 10 6 2

OPENER	RESPONDER
1NT	2♥
2♠	2NT
PASS	

With only a doubleton spade, opener elects to play in notrump rather than spades. With a minimum, 15 points, opener declines the invitation and the partnership stops in partscore in notrump.

Let's change opener's hand:

OPENER	RESPONDER
♠ 5 4	♠ A 10 9 6 3
♥ A K J 3	♥ Q 4
♦ A 10 9 5	♦ 7 3
♣ K Q 7	♣ J 10 6 2

OPENER	RESPONDER
1NT	2♥
2♠	2NT
3NT	PASS

The auction begins as before, but with a maximum, 17 points, opener accepts the invitation. With only two spades, opener chooses to play game in notrump.

Let's change opener's hand again:

OPENER	RESPONDER
♠ K 5 4	♠ A 10 9 6 3
♥ A K 8 3	♥ Q 4
♦ 10 9 5	♦ 7 3
♣ K Q 7	♣ J 10 6 2

OPENER	RESPONDER
1NT	2♥
2♠	2NT
3♠	PASS

This time opener has three-card support for spades and decides to play with spades as trumps. With a minimum, opener elects to play in partscore.

One final change:

OPENER	RESPONDER
♠ K Q 4	♠ A 10 9 6 3
♥ A K 8 3	♥ Q 4
♦ 10 9 5	♦ 7 3
♣ K Q 7	♣ J 10 6 2

OPENER	RESPONDER
1NT	2♥
2♠	2NT
4♠	PASS

With both a fit for spades and a maximum, opener bids game in spades.

Using Transfers When Responder Has a Weak Hand of 0–7 Points

With 0–7 points, responder knows How High the partnership belongs, partscore. Even if opener has a maximum, 17 points, the partnership has at most 24 combined points (17 + 7). The only decision is Where.

WHEN RESPONDER HAS A SIX-CARD OR LONGER MAJOR SUIT

With a six-card or longer major suit, responder knows Where. The partnership belongs in partscore in the major. Responder simply transfers to the major and passes.

For example, these might be the combined hands:

Opener	Responder
♠ A K 6 4	♠ 8 7 2
♥ J 8	♥ 10 9 7 5 3 2
♦ A 9 5	♦ 6
♣ Q J 10 7	♣ 9 4 3

Opener	Responder
1NT	2♦
2♥	Pass

In 1NT, the best declarer could hope for is to promote two club winners to go with the ♠A–K and ♦A. The defenders, however, may be able to develop their winners first. So, 1NT will be defeated at least two tricks, likely more. In 2♥, declarer has a chance. Declarer might be able to promote three heart tricks and two club tricks to go with the ♠A–K and ♦A, for a total of eight tricks. At worst, the contract is unlikely to be defeated by more than one trick.

WHEN RESPONDER HAS A FIVE-CARD MAJOR SUIT

With only a five-card major suit, responder cannot be sure that there is an eight-card major suit fit. With a weak hand, responder has a dilemma. There's not enough room on the Bidding Ladder to bring opener into the decision on whether to play in notrump or the major suit. Responder simply has to make the decision. On balance, responder should transfer to a five-card major suit with a weak hand. Opener may have three-card or longer support, and even if opener has only two cards in the suit, playing in the major may work out best. For example, these might be the combined hands:

OPENER	RESPONDER
♠ J 2	♠ Q 10 9 6 3
♥ Q 7 3	♥ 8
♦ A K 9 8	♦ 7 6 5 2
♣ K Q 7 2	♣ 8 4 3

OPENER	RESPONDER
1NT	2♥
2♠	PASS

In 1NT, declarer has only two sure tricks in diamonds. Declarer can promote a trick in clubs and might get another trick through length in diamonds. Any other tricks will have to come from a favorable lie of the cards or help from the defense. Declarer can't make much use of dummy's spade suit. Even though three tricks could be promoted by driving out the ♠A and ♠K, there is no way to get to them.

In 2♠, even though it is a seven-card fit, declarer is better placed. Declarer will get three tricks from the spade suit in responder's hand and might be able to scramble seven or eight tricks.

Stayman or Transfers?

How does responder know whether to use Stayman or a transfer bid? The guideline is that responder should use Stayman when holding a 4-card major, even with another 5-card or longer major, but use a transfer when holding a 5-card or longer major but no 4-card major. The following chart summarizes responder's choices:

Number of cards in the major suit	Responder's Point Range		
	0-7 points	8 or 9 points	10-15 points
6 or more cards	Transfer & pass	Transfer & raise the major	Transfer & bid game in the major
5 cards	Transfer & pass	Transfer & bid 2NT	Transfer & bid 3NT
4 cards	Pass	2♣ (Stayman)	2♣ (Stayman)
3 or fewer cards	Pass	2NT	3NT

For example, consider these two hands:

OPENER	RESPONDER
♠ Q J 8 3	♠ K 10 9 4
♥ 10 5	♥ J 9 7 6 4 2
♦ A Q J 7	♦ K 5
♣ A K 3	♣ 6

OPENER	RESPONDER
1NT	2♣
2♠	4♠
PASS	

The 4♠ contract has a good chance of success. Declarer can promote three spade tricks to go with the four diamond tricks and two club tricks. Declarer can get a tenth trick by trumping a club in the dummy, responder's hand.

A 4♥ contract would have no chance. The defenders would get the ♠A and the ♥A–K–Q. So, using Stayman when holding a four-card major works better on these combined hands than transferring opener to hearts and raising to 4♥.

Signing Off in a Minor Suit

When opener bids 1NT, a response of 2♣ is the Stayman convention and a response of 2♦ is a transfer bid to 2♥. So what does responder do with a weak hand and a long club or diamond suit? Many partnerships that use Jacoby transfer bids extend the concept to give responder a method for signing off in a minor suit:

Signing off in a Minor Suit

After an opening bid of 1NT, a response of 2♠ asks opener to bid 3♣. Responder then:

- Passes to sign off in a partscore in clubs.
- Bids 3♦ to sign off in a partscore in diamonds (which opener will pass).

The downside of this approach is that the partnership has to play partscore at the three level in a minor suit rather than the two level. This is considered to be a small price to pay for the advantages of using the Stayman convention and Jacoby transfers. Another disadvantage is that responder will be the declarer in a diamond contract rather than opener[27].

---

[27] There are other approaches that can be used for signing off in a minor suit, but they are outside the scope of this book.

OPENER	RESPONDER
♠ J 9 7 6	♠ 4
♥ A K 7 5	♥ 6 3
♦ K Q	♦ J 9 7 6 5 3 2
♣ A 7 3	♣ 8 5 4

OPENER	RESPONDER
1NT	2♠
3♣	3♦
PASS	

With only 1 high-card point, responder knows the partnership belongs in partscore but 1NT would be a poor contract. So responder bids 2♠ to ask opener to bid 3♣ and then bids 3♦, which opener is expected to pass.

Inviting Game with a Minor Suit

With about 8 or 9 points and a six-card or longer minor suit, responder can jump to 3♣ or 3♦ as an invitational bid, asking opener to pass with a minimum or bid game with a maximum[28].

OPENER	RESPONDER
♠ A 7 4	♠ 9 2
♥ K Q 9 7	♥ J 8 3
♦ K Q 8 5	♦ 7 4
♣ J 3	♣ A Q 10 8 7 5

OPENER	RESPONDER
1NT	3♣
PASS	

With 7 high-card points plus 2 length points for the six-card club suit, responder is unsure whether the partnership has enough

[28] There are other approaches that can be used for inviting in a minor suit but, they are outside the scope of this book.

combined strength for game. Responder makes an invitational jump to 3♣ and opener, with a minimum hand, passes. The partnership stops safely in partscore with clubs as the trump suit.

OPENER	RESPONDER
♠ A 7 4	♠ 9 2
♥ A K 9 7	♥ 8 4
♦ A 7	♦ K Q 8 6 4 2
♣ Q 8 6 2	♣ J 9 5

OPENER	RESPONDER
1NT	3♦
3NT	PASS

With 6 high-card points plus 2 length points for the six-card diamond suit, responder has enough to invite the partnership to game. Responder makes an invitational jump to 3♦. With a maximum, opener accepts the invitation by bidding 3NT. It should be easier to make game in notrump than in 5♦, which would require eleven tricks rather than nine.

Other Considerations for Jacoby Transfers

Although the most common use of Jacoby transfer bids occurs when responding to an opening bid of 1NT, most partnerships use transfers after a notrump overcall or higher-level notrump opening bids.

Using Transfers After a Notrump Overcall

Transfers can be used after any natural notrump overcall:

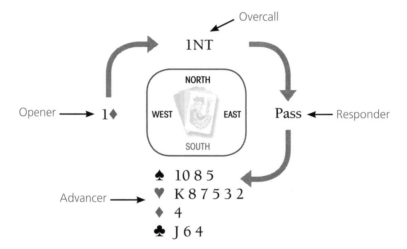

2♦. North's 1NT overcall shows a balanced hand similar to an opening bid of 1NT. South, as advancer, can use a Jacoby transfer bid to put the partnership in a partscore contract of 2♥. The 2♦ bid asks North to bid 2♥ which advancer will then pass[29].

---

[29] It's important for the partnership to have an agreement about using Stayman and transfer bids after notrump overcalls. Otherwise, the partnership is likely to have a bidding misunderstanding.

After a Higher-Level Opening Notrump Bid

Transfers are so useful that they are also used after a 2NT opening bid[30], together with Stayman. This is discussed further in the next chapter.

Responder's Bids Over 2NT

- 3♥ Jacoby transfer to spades
- 3♦ Jacoby transfer to hearts
- 3♣ Stayman

When the Opponents Interfere

If the opponents double 1NT, no bidding room has been taken up so transfers can still be used.

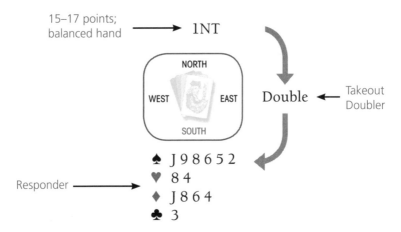

2♥. East's double doesn't prevent responder from bidding 2♥ as a transfer to ask opener to bid 2♠. South will then pass, leaving the partnership in partscore.

---

[30] Transfers and Stayman are also used after the auction begins 2♣ - 2♦ - 2NT. See Chapter 3.

If an opponent overcalls after the 1NT opening, a popular agreement is that transfers are off and all bids are natural[31]. For example:

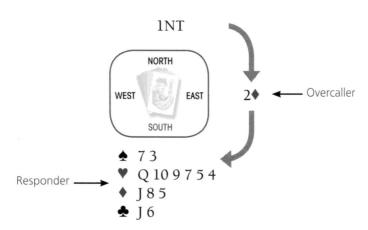

1NT

NORTH
WEST   EAST
SOUTH

2♦ ⟵ Overcaller

Responder ⟶
♠ 7 3
♥ Q 10 9 7 5 4
♦ J 8 5
♣ J 6

2♥. 2♥ is a natural, non-forcing bid, not a transfer to spades. To make a forcing bid, responder would jump to 3♥. A double of 2♦ would be for penalty.

If an opponent interferes after responder has made a transfer bid, opener can judge whether or not to accept the transfer.

NORTH WEST EAST SOUTH	WEST	NORTH	EAST	SOUTH
	1NT	PASS	2♦	DOUBLE
	?			

♠ A 4
♥ K 7 2
♦ K Q 8 6 5
♣ K 10 2

2♥. South's double doesn't prevent West from accepting the transfer. With three-card support for hearts, West knows the partnership has an eight-card fit and is happy to accept the transfer.

---

[31] Some players continue to use transfers after a 2♣ overcall.

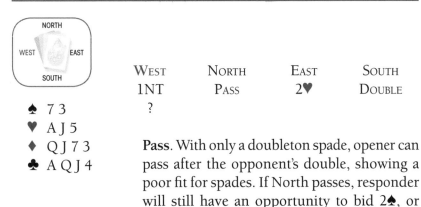

WEST	NORTH	EAST	SOUTH
1NT	PASS	2♥	DOUBLE
?			

♠ 7 3
♥ A J 5
♦ Q J 7 3
♣ A Q J 4

Pass. With only a doubleton spade, opener can pass after the opponent's double, showing a poor fit for spades. If North passes, responder will still have an opportunity to bid 2♠, or may choose another suit, knowing opener doesn't particularly like spa...

WEST	NORTH	EAST	SOUTH
1NT	PASS	2♦	2♠
?			

♠ A 4
♥ K 7 2
♦ K Q 8 6 5
♣ K 10 2

Pass. South's overcall takes away opener's obligation to bid hearts. Although opener knows the partnership has an eight-card heart fit, responder may have a weak hand. West passes, leaving any further decision to responder. Opener would typically judge to bid 3♥ only with a maximum and four-card support for hearts.

Responder's Immediate Jump in a Major Suit

If the partnership does not use Jacoby transfer bids, responder's jump to 3♥ or 3♠ after an opening 1NT bid is forcing, asking opener to choose between 3NT and game in the major suit. Once the partnership adopts transfer bids, responder would transfer to the major and then jump to 3NT to ask opener to choose between 3NT and game in the major. As a result, responder's jump to 3♥ or 3♠ can be assigned a different meaning.

A popular agreement is to use a responder's jump to 3♥ or 3♠ to show a good six-card or longer suit and interest in reaching a slam

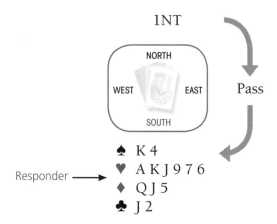

1NT

NORTH

WEST   EAST   Pass

SOUTH

♠ K 4
Responder ⟶ ♥ A K J 9 7 6
♦ Q J 5
♣ J 2

contract—about 16 or more points. For example:
3♥. With 15 high-card points plus 2 length points for the six-card heart suit, responder is too strong to simply transfer to hearts and bid game. The jump to 3♥ shows interest in bigger things. Opener can bid 3NT with poor support for hearts and a minimum opening bid. Responder will then likely settle for game. With a fit for hearts, opener can raise to 4♥ and the partnership will likely get to 6♥. Slam bidding is discussed in more detail in Chapter 4. For now, this is simply included here for completeness.

What about an immediate jump to 4♥ or 4♠ by responder over partner's 1NT opening bid? For now, these can simply be treated as natural responses by responder, showing a six-card or longer suit with enough strength for game. However, since responder could transfer to the major suit and then raise to game with this type of hand, some partnerships prefer to assign a different meaning to such jumps. See the discussion of Texas transfer bids in Appendix 2.

SUMMARY

When responding to 1NT, the partnership can use both Stayman and Jacoby transfer bids.

Responding to 1NT

Responder	3NT	To play (10+ points)
	3♠/♥	Forcing (6+ card suit, slam interest)
	3♣/♦	Invitational (6+ card suit and 8–9 points)
	2NT	Invitational (8–9 points)
	2♠	Transfer bid to 3♣ (to play in 3♣ or 3♦)
	2♥	Transfer bid to 2♠
	2♦	Transfer bid to 2♥
	2♣	Stayman

1NT

Opener   15–17 points; balanced hand

Opener's Rebid

- In reply to a transfer bid of 2♦, opener bids 2♥; in reply to a transfer bid of 2♥, opener bids 2♠.
- In reply to a transfer bid of 2♠, opener bids 3♣ and then passes if responder bids 3♦.
- In reply to responder's invitational bid of 2NT, 3♣ or 3♦, opener passes with a minimum and bids 3NT with a maximum.

Responder's Rebid After Using a Jacoby Transfer Bid

Number of cards in the major suit	Responder's Point Range		
	0–7 points	8 or 9 points	10–15 points
6 or more cards	Transfer & pass	Transfer & raise	Transfer & bid game
5 cards	Transfer & pass	Transfer & bid 2NT	Transfer & bid 3NT

Other Considerations for Jacoby Transfer

AFTER A 1NT OVERCALL

Jacoby transfers can be used by advancer after a 1NT overcall.

AFTER HIGHER-LEVEL NOTRUMP OPENING BIDS AND OVERCALLS

Jacoby transfers can be used after higher-level notrump opening bids and overcalls.

WHEN THE OPPONENTS INTERFERE

Here are popular agreements after responder's right-hand opponent interferes:

Right-hand Opponent's Action	Responder's Action
Double	Transfers are still in effect
Overcall	Transfers no longer apply

Quiz – Part I

North is the dealer and opens 1NT. East passes. What response does South make with each of the following hands? What is South's plan?

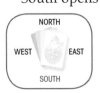

WEST	NORTH	EAST	SOUTH
	1NT	PASS	?

a) ♠ 4
   ♥ J 10 8 7 5 3
   ♦ Q 8 3 2
   ♣ 9 8

b) ♠ K J 9 6 5 4
   ♥ 8 3
   ♦ K 6
   ♣ 7 4 2

c) ♠ A K
   ♥ 10 9 7 6 5 2
   ♦ K 7 6
   ♣ 5 4

d) ♠ Q J 6 4 2
   ♥ Q 8 3
   ♦ 8 4 2
   ♣ K 6

e) ♠ K Q 6
   ♥ A 10 8 5 2
   ♦ 10 3
   ♣ Q 4 3

f) ♠ 7 6 2
   ♥ 8 5
   ♦ 4
   ♣ Q 10 8 7 5 3 2

South opens 1NT with this hand: ♠ 9 2
                                 ♥ A Q 4
                                 ♦ K J 8 6 5
                                 ♣ K Q 9

What rebid does South make in each of the following auctions?

g)

WEST	NORTH	EAST	SOUTH
			1NT
PASS	2♦	PASS	?

h)

WEST	NORTH	EAST	SOUTH
			1NT
PASS	2♥	PASS	?

i)

WEST	NORTH	EAST	SOUTH
			1NT
PASS	2♠	PASS	?

Answers to Quiz – Part I

a) 2♦. This is a transfer to 2♥. When opener bids 2♥, South will pass, putting the partnership in partscore in hearts.

b) 2♥. This is a transfer to 2♠. After opener bids 2♠, South plans to raise to 3♠ as an invitation.

c) 2♦. This is a transfer to 2♥. When opener bids 2♥, South will raise to 4♥ to put the partnership in game in hearts.

d) 2♥. This is a transfer to 2♠. South plans to then bid 2NT, inviting opener to game in either notrump or spades.

e) 2♦. This is a transfer to 2♥. South then plans to jump to 3NT to ask opener to choose between 3NT and 4♥.

f) 2♠. This asks opener to bid 3♣. South will then pass, leaving the partnership to play in a partscore in clubs.

g) 2♥. Responder's 2♦ bid asks opener to bid hearts. Opener simply accepts responder's request.

h) 2♠. Responder's 2♥ bid is a transfer to spades. Opener bids 2♠, as requested. Responder isn't asking whether opener likes spades. Opener simply follows instructions.

i) 3♣. The 2♠ bids asks opener to bid 3♣. Responder may be planning to pass—leaving the partnership to play partscore in clubs—or may be planning to bid 3♦, putting the partnership in partscore with diamonds as the trump suit.

Quiz – Part II

North opens 1NT, South responds 2♥ and North bids 2♠. What call would South make with each of the following hands?

WEST	NORTH	EAST	SOUTH
	1NT	PASS	2♥
PASS	2♠	PASS	?

a) ♠ 9 7 6 5 3 2
♥ J 8 4
♦ 7 2
♣ 10 6

b) ♠ K J 8 7 5 3
♥ 7 2
♦ K 9 4
♣ 8 5

c) ♠ Q 10 9 7 6 4 3
♥ A 8
♦ 9 5
♣ Q 7

d) ♠ A Q 8 6 3
♥ Q 7 2
♦ 9 8 4
♣ 6 5

e) ♠ Q J 8 6 3
♥ 9 5
♦ A Q 8 3
♣ Q 4

f) ♠ J 8 7 5 3
♥ 9
♦ J 10 7 3
♣ K 8 2

South opens 1NT, North responds 2♦, South bids 2♥, and North now bids 2NT. What call would South make with each of the following hands?

WEST	NORTH	EAST	SOUTH
			1NT
PASS	2♦	PASS	2♥
PASS	2NT	PASS	?

g) ♠ A Q 8 5
♥ 8 3
♦ K J 7 5
♣ K Q 7

h) ♠ A 10 8
♥ Q 5
♦ A K 10 5
♣ K J 9 7

i) ♠ Q 9
♥ K 10 5
♦ A J 8 3
♣ K Q 7 2

j) ♠ K Q 6 2
♥ A J 5
♦ A 9 7 3
♣ K 4

k) ♠ Q J 8 7
♥ 9 4
♦ K Q 3
♣ A K J 5

l) ♠ A Q J
♥ Q 10 7 3
♦ J 10 9 3
♣ A Q

Answers to Quiz – Part II

a) **Pass**. South knows **How High**—partscore—and **Where**—spades—the partnership belongs. Using transfer bids, South transfers opener to spades and then passes.

b) **3♠**. With 7 high-card points plus 2 length points for the six-card spade suit, South has enough to invite game. South transfers opener to spades and then raises.

c) **4♠**. With 8 high-card points plus 3 length points for the seven-card suit, South knows there is enough combined strength for game. South also knows the partnership belongs in spades.

d) **2NT**. With 8 high-card points plus 1 length point for the five-card suit, South starts by transferring opener to spades to show the five-card suit. South then follows with 2NT to invite game. Opener can now decide whether to play in partscore or game and whether to play in spades or notrump.

e) **3NT**. With 11 high-card points plus 1 length point for the five-card spade suit, South has enough to take the partnership to game. Unsure whether there is an eight-card spade fit, South transfers to spades and then jumps to 3NT, asking opener to choose between game in spades and game in notrump.

f) **Pass**. With a weak hand and a five-card major suit, responder transfers to the major and then passes.

g) **Pass**. Responder is showing an invitational-strength hand with a five-card heart suit. With a minimum and only two hearts, South passes.

h) **3NT**. With a maximum 17 points, opener accepts the invitation. With only two hearts, opener chooses to play in notrump.

i) **3♥**. With a minimum, 15 points, opener declines the invitation to bid game. With three-card support for hearts, opener chooses to play partscore in the eight-card heart fit.

j) **4♥**. With three-card support for hearts and a maximum, 17 points, opener accepts the invitation and the partnership goes to game in hearts.

k) **Pass (3NT)**. With 16 points, opener is on the borderline of accepting the invitation. With a poor fit for hearts, opener would probably decide to play in partscore rather than game.

l) **4♥**. With 16 points opener could choose to decline the invitation and play in partscore. However, with an excellent fit for hearts, most players would accept the invitation and take the partnership to game.

Quiz – Part III

South bids 1NT with this hand:　♠ Q 4
　　　　　　　　　　　　　　　　♥ A J 7 5
　　　　　　　　　　　　　　　　♦ 9 5 2
　　　　　　　　　　　　　　　　♣ A K J 4

What call does South make in each of the following auctions?

a)

WEST	NORTH	EAST	SOUTH
			1NT
PASS	2♥	PASS	2♠
PASS	3NT	PASS	?

b)

West	North	East	South
			1NT
PASS	2♠	PASS	3♣
PASS	3♦	PASS	?

c)

WEST	NORTH	EAST	SOUTH
			1NT
PASS	2♥	3♦	?

d)

WEST	NORTH	EAST	SOUTH
			1NT
PASS	2♦	DOUBLE	?

e)

WEST	NORTH	EAST	SOUTH
		1♣	1NT
PASS	2♥	PASS	?

Answers to Quiz – Part III

a) **Pass**. By transferring to spades and then jumping to 3NT, responder is asking opener to choose between game in notrump or in spades. With only two spades, opener would choose to play game in notrump.

b) **Pass**. Responder's 2♠ bid asks opener to bid 3♣. Responder's subsequent 3♦ bid says responder would like to play partscore in diamonds.

c) **Pass**. North's 2♥ bid asks opener to bid 2♠, but when East interferes, opener does not have to bid. With a minimum and poor support for spades, opener takes advantage of the opportunity to pass.

d) **2♥**. North's 2♦ response asks opener to bid 2♥. After East doubles, South doesn't have to bid, but with excellent support for hearts, South should accept the transfer.

e) **2♠**. Here South has overcalled 1NT. Most partnerships play transfer bids after a notrump overcall, so North's 2♥ bid is a transfer to spades. South bids 2♠ as asked by North.

DEAL: 5	♠	10 7
	♥	A K J 5
DEALER: NORTH	♦	K 8 3
VUL: NONE	♣	K Q J 3

WEST		EAST
♠ A 8 4 2	NORTH	♠ K
♥ Q 7 4	WEST EAST	♥ 10 9 8 3 2
♦ Q J 10		♦ A 9 6 2
♣ 9 6 5	SOUTH	♣ A 10 8

♠ Q J 9 6 5 3
♥ 6
♦ 7 5 4
♣ 7 4 2

Suggested Bidding

WEST	NORTH	EAST	SOUTH
	1NT	PASS	2♥
PASS	2♠	PASS	PASS
PASS			

With a balanced hand and 17 high-card points, North opens 1NT.

With 3 high-card points plus 2 length points for the six-card spade suit, South has the answer to How High, partscore. The partnership has at most 22 combined points (17 + 5). South also has the answer to Where, spades. South has a six-card spade suit and North must have at least two spades, so the partnership has an eight-card or longer major suit fit.

Using Jacoby transfer bids, South responds 2♥, asking opener to bid 2♠. After North dutifully bids 2♠, South passes, leaving the partnership playing partscore in spades with North as the declarer.

Suggested Opening Lead

Against a suit contract, it is usually not a good idea to lead a low card from a suit headed by the ace. It is also risky to lead an ace without the king in the same suit. So, East would lead the ♥10, top of the solid sequence in hearts.

Declarer's Plan

Declarer starts by Assessing the situation. North's goal is to take 8 tricks. There are two sure heart tricks.

North can plan to promote four winners in the spade suit and two tricks in the club suit. Once East leads a heart, declarer is guaranteed an extra winner in that suit with the ♥J whether or not West plays the ♥Q. Declarer can develop enough tricks to make the contract but, when

```
┌─── DECLARER'S PLAN—THE ABC'S ───┐

  Declarer: North     Contract: 2♠

  ASSESS THE SITUATION
    Goal                      8
    Sure Tricks               2
    Extra Tricks Needed   6

  BROWSE DECLARER'S CHECKLIST
    Promotion             4 in spades
                          2 in clubs
    Length
    The Finesse
    Trumping in Dummy

  CONSIDER THE ORDER
    • Discard potential diamond losers.
    • Draw trumps.
```

Considering the Order, declarer must be aware of the potential tricks the defenders can take[12]. If West gains the lead, the defenders might be able to take three diamond tricks by trapping North's ♦K when East has the ♦A. To prevent this, declarer should take the extra heart winners and discard diamonds from dummy before leading trumps. After the opening lead, declarer has two more heart winners to take and can discard two of South's diamonds. Now the defenders cannot take more than one diamond trick on gaining the lead.

Declarer can now lead spades to drive out the defenders' ♠K and ♠A and draw the remainder of the defenders' trumps. Finally, declarer can drive out the ♣A to promote two winners in that suit.

Comments

North-South do well to play with spades as the trump suit and with North, the stronger hand, as the declarer. If South were declarer in a contract of 2♠, West could lead the ♦Q and the defenders would take the first three diamond tricks since North's ♦K is trapped. The defenders would also get tricks with the ♠A-K and ♣A to defeat the contract one trick. By using the Jacoby transfer to protect North's high cards, North-South reach a makeable partscore contract.

---

[12] The danger from the opponents is discussed in Appendix 1 on declarer play.

DEAL: 6

DEALER: EAST
VUL: N-S

```
              ♠ Q J 10 9 2
              ♥ J 9
              ♦ 9 4
              ♣ K J 10 5

    ♠ A 5           NORTH        ♠ K 8 6 3
    ♥ 8 7 6 5 3 2              ♥ A 4
    ♦ A 6 2     WEST    EAST    ♦ K 7 3
    ♣ 8 4                       ♣ A Q 6 2
                   SOUTH

              ♠ 7 4
              ♥ K Q 10
              ♦ Q J 10 8 5
              ♣ 9 7 3
```

Suggested Bidding

WEST	NORTH	EAST	SOUTH
		1NT	PASS
2♦	PASS	2♥	PASS
4♥	PASS	PASS	PASS

East opens 1NT with a balanced hand and 16 high-card points. South passes.

With 8 high-card points plus 2 length points for the six-card heart suit, West knows How High the partnership belongs, game. The partnership has at least 25 combined points (15 + 10 = 25). West also knows the partnership has at least an eight-card heart fit since opener must have at least two hearts to have a balanced hand. West therefore knows Where, hearts. West doesn't worry about the quality of the heart suit; the only consideration is that the partnership has at least an eight-card fit. Knowing How High and Where, West wants to put the partnership in a game contract of 4♥.

Using Jacoby transfer bids, West starts by bidding 2♦, telling opener to bid 2♥. After opener bids 2♥, West raises to 4♥ to put the partnership in a game contract played by the 1NT opener, East.

Suggested Opening Lead

South leads the ♦Q, top of the solid sequence.

Declarer's Plan

East's goal is to take at least ten tricks to make 4♥. East counts sure winners: two spades, one heart, two diamonds, and one club, for a total of six. Four more tricks are needed.

East browses Declarer's Checklist. The heart suit can provide three extra tricks through length if the five missing hearts are divided 3-2. Also, the club suit might provide an extra trick with the help of a finesse.

In considering the order in which to do things, declarer can start by developing the extra tricks in hearts. This has the effect of drawing trumps at the same time. Declarer wins the ♦K and plays the ♥A and a second round of hearts, giving up a trick. If the defenders lead another diamond, declarer wins the ♦A and can lead another heart to establish the remaining hearts in dummy as winners[33].

After winning the third round of hearts, South can take the diamond winner, but that will be the last trick for the defense. If South next leads a spade, declarer wins the ♠A and leads a low club toward the ♣A-Q. When North plays a low club, declarer finesses the ♣Q, and proceeds to win the rest of the tricks.

DECLARER'S PLAN—THE ABC'S

Declarer: East   Contract: 4♥

ASSESS THE SITUATION

Goal	10
Sure Tricks	6
Extra Tricks Needed	4

BROWSE DECLARER'S CHECKLIST

Promotion	
Length	3 in hearts
The Finesse	1 in clubs
Trumping in Dummy	

CONSIDER THE ORDER

- Draw trumps, taking losses early.
- Use an entry to dummy to take the club finesse.

Comments

East-West can make 4♥ but not 3NT. Against 3NT, South would lead diamonds at each opportunity. Declarer will have to establish winners in hearts, but South will win the race, establishing three diamond winners to go with two hearts. With six hearts, West should focus on the length of the suit, not the strength. An eight-card major suit fit will usually be a better spot than notrump.

---

[33] Declarer doesn't actually have to drive out the defenders' last trump. Declarer can let the defenders take it whenever they wish and go about taking and developing other tricks at this point.

DEAL: 7
DEALER: SOUTH
VUL: E-W

NORTH
♠ 9 6
♥ Q 6 3
♦ K J 9 5 4 2
♣ J 6

WEST
♠ K J 5
♥ A K 7 5
♦ 7 3
♣ A 10 7 2

EAST
♠ Q 10 8 4 3
♥ 8 4
♦ A 8
♣ K 8 4 3

SOUTH
♠ A 7 2
♥ J 10 9 2
♦ Q 10 6
♣ Q 9 5

Suggested Bidding

WEST	NORTH	EAST	SOUTH
			PASS
1NT	PASS	2♥	PASS
2♠	PASS	3NT	PASS
4♠	PASS	PASS	PASS

West opens 1NT with 15 high-card points and a balanced hand. North does not have a good enough suit or enough strength to overcall at the two level.

East has 9 high-card points plus 1 length point for the five-card spade suit. The total of 10 points is enough to give East the answer to HOW HIGH. There should be enough combined strength for game even if West has a minimum of 15 points. However, East isn't sure about WHERE. If West has three or more spades, the partnership has an eight-card or longer major suit fit and 4♠ should be the best spot; if West has only two spades, 3NT will likely be the best spot.

East starts by making a transfer bid of 2♥. After West dutifully bids 2♠, East jumps to 3NT. This asks West to choose between 3NT and 4♠. East has shown a five-card spade suit—by using the transfer bid of 2♥—and enough strength to want to be in a game contract by jumping to 3NT.

With three spades, West knows the partnership has an eight-card spade suit and chooses to play in 4♠ rather than 3NT. West's 4♠ bid is followed by three passes.

Suggested Opening Lead

North doesn't have a clear lead against 4♠. With nothing else particularly attractive, North might choose the ♦5, fourth highest.

Declarer's Plan

West's goal is to take at least ten tricks. West can count on two sure tricks in hearts, one in diamonds, and two in clubs. That's a total of five tricks, five short of the goal.

Four tricks can be promoted in spades. A fifth trick can be developed through length in clubs if the five missing clubs are divided 3-2.

```
┌──── DECLARER'S PLAN—THE ABC'S ────┐

Declarer: West      Contract: 4♠

ASSESS THE SITUATION
   Goal                      10
   Sure Tricks                5
   Extra Tricks Needed        5

BROWSE DECLARER'S CHECKLIST
   Promotion            4 in spades
   Length               1 in clubs
   The Finesse
   Trumping in Dummy

CONSIDER THE ORDER
   • Draw trumps.
   • Take the loss early in the club suit.
```

After winning the ♦A, declarer's priority is to draw trumps. Declarer drives out the ♠A. When South wins the ♠A, the defenders can take a diamond, but whatever they lead next, declarer can win and draw trumps.

Next, declarer can establish a club winner by playing the ♣A, ♣K, and a third round of clubs, losing a trick to South's ♣Q. Declarer's fourth club is now a winner. By taking the loss early, before taking both heart winners and all the spade winners, declarer can regain the lead no matter what South leads after winning the ♣Q.

Comments

East-West do well to reach 4♠. If East-West were in 3NT, North would lead a diamond and drive out the ♦A. On winning the ♠A, the defenders can take their established diamonds and defeat the contract two tricks. The use of the transfer bid lets the partnership uncover their eight-card spade fit and reach the best game contract.

DEAL: 8
DEALER: WEST
VUL: BOTH

♠ K 7 6
♥ A 9 7 6 3
♦ J 7 2
♣ 5 4

♠ J 10 9 5 3
♥ K 5
♦ A 8
♣ J 9 7 2

NORTH
WEST EAST
SOUTH

♠ 8 2
♥ Q J 10 2
♦ K 6 4 3
♣ Q 10 6

♠ A Q 4
♥ 8 4
♦ Q 10 9 5
♣ A K 8 3

Suggested Bidding

WEST	NORTH	EAST	SOUTH
PASS	PASS	PASS	1NT
PASS	2♦	PASS	2♥
PASS	2NT	PASS	PASS
PASS			

After three passes, South opens 1NT with 15 high-card points and a balanced hand. West passes.

North is unsure about both HOW HIGH and WHERE the partnership belongs. With 8 high-card points plus 1 length point for the five-card heart suit, North wants to invite the partnership to game. North also wants to find out if the partnership has an eight-card or longer heart fit. To accomplish both objectives, North starts by bidding 2♦ as a transfer to hearts. After South bids 2♥, North now rebids 2NT.

North's sequence of bids shows an invitational strength hand with a five-card heart suit, leaving South to decide the best contract. With a minimum for the 1NT opening, South wants to stop in partscore. With only a doubleton heart, South prefers to play in notrump rather than hearts. So, South passes, leaving the partnership in a partscore in notrump.

Suggested Opening Lead

West makes the opening lead. West would lead the ♠J, top of the solid sequence in the longest suit.

Declarer's Plan

South is declarer and the goal is to take eight tricks. South counts three sure tricks in spades, one in hearts, and two in clubs. Two more tricks need to be developed.

Browsing Declarer's Checklist, there is an opportunity to promote two winners in the diamond suit. There is also the possibility of getting extra tricks through length in the

```
┌ DECLARER'S PLAN—THE ABC'S ┐
 Declarer: South   Contract: 2NT
 ASSESS THE SITUATION
   Goal                    8
   Sure Tricks             6
   Extra Tricks Needed     2
 BROWSE DECLARER'S CHECKLIST
   Promotion        2 in diamonds
   Length
   The Finesse
   Trumping in Dummy
 CONSIDER THE ORDER
   • Take the losses early in diamonds.
```

heart suit if the missing hearts divide 3-3 or 4-2, but the diamonds offer a sure thing.

Suppose declarer wins the first trick with the ♠Q. Declarer should start developing the extra diamond winners right away. Declarer starts by playing a low diamond to dummy's ♦J, high card from the short side first. Suppose East wins the ♦K and leads another spade. Declarer wins and leads another diamond to drive out West's ♦A. West can lead another spade to drive out declarer's last winner in the suit, but now declarer has enough tricks: three spades, one heart, two diamonds, and two clubs.

Comments

Transfer bids help the partnership decide both HOW HIGH and WHERE the contract belongs. On this deal, the partnership managed to stop in partscore and also determine that there was no eight-card fit in hearts.

Nearly every system employs some special opening bid to show an unusually powerful hand, a hand that will produce game by itself or with the most meager support—including unbiddable support—from partner, and a hand that gives high hopes of a slam if partner has anything better than that.

—Albert Morehead, Morehead on Bidding (1964)

Strong Opening Bids

Suppose you have an opportunity to open the bidding and this is your hand:

♠ A K Q J 10 9 8
♥ A K
♦ A Q 3
♣ 4

If you open 1♠ and partner passes, you would be disappointed. Even if partner has nothing, you have enough strength to make 4♠. The problem is that an opening bid at the one level is not forcing. Responder can pass with fewer than 6 points, which is quite likely when you have this much power.

One consideration might be to open 4♠ to be sure to get to game. The disadvantage of this approach is that it takes up a lot of room on the Bidding Ladder and will make it difficult for the partnership to investigate the possibility of going for a slam bonus. If partner holds as little as the ♦K, you will be able to take twelve tricks: seven spade tricks, two heart tricks, and three diamond tricks. When you have a hand as strong as this, a slam contract is quite likely, but partner would not want to venture beyond the game level with only the ♦K.

At one time, an opening bid of 2♠ was used to show this type of hand, a hand too strong to open at the one level where we want responder to bid even with a very weak hand. The modern style is to use an opening bid of 2♠ as a weak two-bid, showing a good six-card suit but fewer than 13 points[34]. Another bid is needed.

The Strong Artificial 2♣ Opening

Only 2♦, 2♥, and 2♠ are used as weak two-bids. 2♣ is reserved for hands that are so strong that opener wants responder to bid, even with no points:

> ### Strong Artificial 2♣ Opening
>
> All strong hands of about 22 or more points are opened 2♣.

The 2♣ bid is artificial because it has nothing to do with clubs. It is simply a forcing bid, telling responder you have a very strong hand.

Here are hands that could be opened with a strong artificial 2♣:

♠ 8
♥ A K J 8 6
♦ A K Q 8 3
♣ A 6

2♣. The hand is worth 23 points, 21 high-card points plus 1 length point for each five-card suit. That's enough strength to open with the artificial 2♣ bid.

♠ A
♥ K Q J 9 8 7 3
♦ 6
♣ A K Q 8

2♣. There are 19 high-card points plus 3 length points for the seven-card suit. That puts this hand into the 2♣ category.

---

[34] See Bridge Basics 2: Competitive Bidding, or the Glossary.

♠ A Q 4	2♣. Balanced hands of 22 or more are opened
♥ K Q J	2♣. This hand has 24 high-card points.
♦ A Q J 2	
♣ K Q 7	

Here are hands that don't meet the guideline for a 2♣ opening bid:

♠ K J 8 6 3	1♠. This is a strong hand, 19 high-card points
♥ A	plus 1 length point for the five-card suit, but
♦ Q 9 7 4	not quite enough to open with a forcing bid.
♣ A K Q	Open 1♠. If partner passes, it's unlikely the
	partnership belongs in a game contract.

♠ 3	1♥/4♥. You are likely to take ten tricks with
♥ A K Q 10 9 8 7 4	no help from partner, eight heart tricks and
♦ Q J 10 9	two diamond tricks through promotion.
♣ —	The hand, however, doesn't have enough
	high-card strength for a 2♣ opening.
	Instead, open 1♥ or a preemptive 4♥ bid.

The requirement of 22 points for an opening 2♣ bid is a guideline, not a rule. Opener can exercise some judgment in deciding whether or not a hand is worth a 2♣ opening bid. For example:

♠ A K Q 10 9 7	2♣. This has 18 high-card points plus 2 length
♥ 5	points for the six-card suit, a total of 20 points.
♦ A K Q 10	However, it is probably worth a 2♣ opening
♣ 6 3	bid since you would expect to take ten tricks,
	six spades and four diamonds, even if partner

has little or no strength. You also have trick-taking potential, with aces and kings, if the opponents were to compete.

♠ K Q 8
♥ A K Q J
♦ K
♣ Q J 7 5 2

1♣. This hand has 21 high-card points plus 1 length point for the five-card suit, a total of 22 points. However, with a poor five-card club suit and a singleton ♦K, this hand is probably not worth opening a strong 2♣. If partner doesn't have enough to bid over a 1♣ opening bid, it's unlikely the partnership can make a game contract.

Responding to a 2♣ Opening Bid

Since the 2♣ opening is artificial, responder can't pass. Opener has not yet had a chance to describe the shape of the hand. To leave opener the maximum room on the Bidding Ladder, responder usually makes an artificial response of 2♦.

The 2♦ Waiting Bid[35]

A response of 2♦ is artificial. It says nothing about responder's strength or distribution. It is simply waiting to hear a further description of opener's hand.

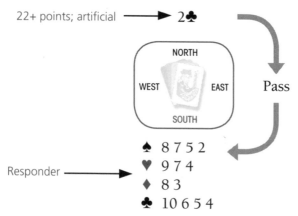

22+ points; artificial ⟶ 2♣

Pass

Responder ⟶

♠ 8 7 5 2
♥ 9 7 4
♦ 8 3
♣ 10 6 5 4

2♦. Even with no points, responder must keep the auction going by using the waiting response of 2♦. If South were to pass, North would be left to play in 2♣, which doesn't promise a club suit!

---

[35] There are many different methods for responding to an artificial 2♣ opening bid. The artificial 2♦ waiting response is the most popular.

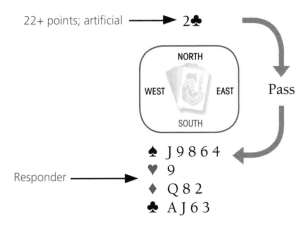

22+ points; artificial ⟶ 2♣

NORTH

WEST   EAST   Pass

SOUTH

♠ J 9 8 6 4
♥ 9
♦ Q 8 2
♣ A J 6 3

Responder ⟶

2♦. With 8 high-card points plus 1 length point for the five-card suit, responder knows the partnership has at least enough combined strength for game, since opener has at least 22 points. However, you want to wait to hear what opener has to say. By responding 2♦, even if opener bids 2♥, for example, showing a strong hand with hearts, you could then bid 2♠ to show your five-card spade suit. If you were to immediately respond 2♠, opener would have to bid 3♥ with a strong heart suit, leaving less room to find the best contract.

Positive Reponses with 8+ Points

Although responder will usually start with the 2♦ waiting bid, there are other options. When responder has about 8 or more high-card points, the partnership will want to consider going for a slam bonus rather than settling for a game. These are referred to as *positive responses*:

> ## Positive Responses
>
> - 2♥, 2♠, 3♣, or 3♦ (not 2♦) show a good five-card suit with two of the top three honors or a six-card or longer suit and 8 or more points.
> - 2NT shows a balanced hand with 8 or more points.

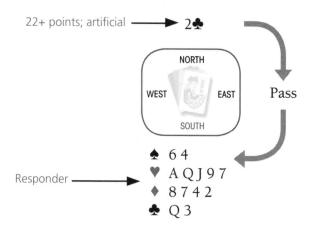

22+ points; artificial ⟶ 2♣

NORTH

WEST   EAST   Pass

SOUTH

♠ 6 4
Responder ⟶ ♥ A Q J 9 7
♦ 8 7 4 2
♣ Q 3

2♥. With a good five-card suit and 9 high-card points, you can make an immediate positive response of 2♥. This shows interest in reaching a slam contract and a potential source of tricks even if opener prefers another suit as trumps.

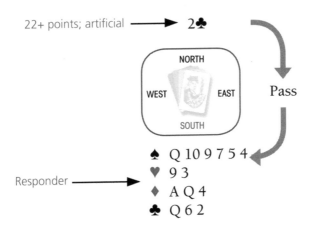

22+ points; artificial ⟶ 2♣

NORTH

WEST   EAST   Pass

SOUTH

Responder ⟶
♠ Q 10 9 7 5 4
♥ 9 3
♦ A Q 4
♣ Q 6 2

2♠. With a six-card suit, you don't need two of the top three honors to make an immediate positive response when you have 8 or more high-card points.

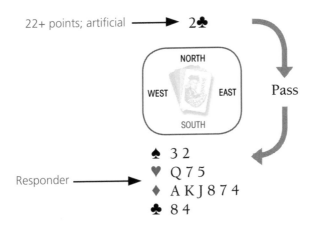

22+ points; artificial ⟶ 2♣

NORTH

WEST   EAST   Pass

SOUTH

Responder ⟶
♠ 3 2
♥ Q 7 5
♦ A K J 8 7 4
♣ 8 4

3♦. To show a positive response with diamonds, responder has to jump to 3♦, since the 2♦ response would be the artificial waiting bid. Responder should use this response sparingly, since it takes up a lot of room on the Bidding Ladder because you are jumping to the three level.

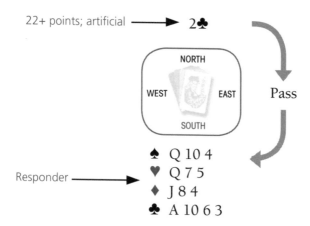

22+ points; artificial ⟶ 2♣

NORTH

WEST   EAST   Pass

SOUTH

Responder ⟶
♠ Q 10 4
♥ Q 7 5
♦ J 8 4
♣ A 10 6 3

2NT. With a balanced hand and 9 high-card points, you can make a positive response. Since it takes bidding room away from opener, many players prefer to respond 2♦ with this type of hand, planning to show the strength later.

Opener's Rebid

After responder makes a waiting response of 2♦, opener makes a descriptive rebid.

Showing an Unbalanced Hand

A rebid in a suit shows an unbalanced hand and is forcing. With an unbalanced hand, opener bids the longest suit or the *higher-ranking* of two five-card or six-card suits.

For example, suppose you are West. You open 2♣ and partner responds 2♦.

WEST	NORTH	EAST	SOUTH
2♣	PASS	2♦	PASS
?			

♠ A
♥ A K Q J 9 7 3
♦ A K 4
♣ 9 3

2♥. After the 2♦ waiting response, you get to show your real suit. There's no need to jump to game, even though you expect to take at least ten tricks. The 2♥ rebid is forcing, so partner must bid again.

WEST	NORTH	EAST	SOUTH
2♣	PASS	2♦	PASS
?			

♠ A K J 10 5
♥ 3
♦ A K Q 9 4
♣ K Q

2♠. With two five-card suits, bid the higher-ranking first. Responder must bid again and you will then have an opportunity to show the second suit.

Showing a Balanced Hand

A rebid in notrump shows a balanced hand and is not forcing. With a balanced hand, opener rebids as follows:

- 2NT   22–24 points
- 3NT   25–27 points
- 4NT   28–30 points...if you are ever so lucky!

For example, suppose you are West. You open 2♣ and partner responds 2♦.

WEST	NORTH	EAST	SOUTH
2♣	PASS	2♦	PASS
?			

♠ A Q 6
♥ A K J
♦ K Q 7
♣ K J 6 3

2NT. With a balanced hand and 23 high-card points, rebid 2NT. This is not forcing. With a very weak hand, responder can pass, knowing you have at most 24 points.

WEST	NORTH	EAST	SOUTH
2♣	PASS	2♦	PASS
?			

♠ K Q J
♥ A K 10
♦ A Q 7 4 3
♣ A Q

3NT. You have 25 high-card points plus 1 length point for the five-card suit. Since the hand is balanced, no void, no singleton, and only one doubleton, a rebid of 3NT is more descriptive than 3♦.

After a Positive Bid by Responder

If responder has bid something other than 2♦, the partnership is committed to at least a game contract, **and looking to reach a slam contract (see next Chapter) if a suitable fit can be found. Opener makes a descriptive rebid.**

For example, suppose you are West. You open 2♣ and partner responds 2♥.

WEST	NORTH	EAST	SOUTH
2♣	PASS	2♥	PASS
?			

♠ A K Q 9 7 6
♥ 4
♦ A K J 3
♣ K 4

2♠. After the positive 2♥ response, the partnership is headed for at least game. The first priority is to find a fit. With no support for hearts, opener shows an unbalanced hand with a five-card or longer spade suit.

WEST	NORTH	EAST	SOUTH
2♣	PASS	2♥	PASS
?			

♠ A Q J 5
♥ Q 4
♦ K Q J 5
♣ A Q J

2NT. You have a balanced hand with 22 high-card points. With only a doubleton heart, describe the hand with a rebid of 2NT, showing 22–24 points and a balanced hand.

	WEST	NORTH	EAST	SOUTH
	2♣	PASS	2♥	PASS
	?			

♠ A K
♥ K 9 6 2
♦ K Q 3
♣ A K J 8

3♥. If responder had bid 2♦, you were planning to describe this hand with a rebid of 2NT, showing a balanced hand of 22–24 points. When responder makes a positive response of 2♥, however, you can raise to show the excellent support. Now that the trump suit has been agreed, the partnership can explore the possibility of a slam contract (see next Chapter).

Responder's Rebid

If responder made a waiting bid of 2♦, the partnership isn't yet committed to reaching game. What happens next depends on opener's rebid.

When Opener Rebids in a Suit

When opener shows an unbalanced hand by opening 2♣ and then bidding a suit, responder can't pass.

WHEN RESPONDER HAS A VERY WEAK HAND OF ABOUT 0–3 POINTS

With a very weak hand, about 0–3 points, responder makes an artificial rebid to tell opener not to expect much help. A popular approach is:

> ## Cheaper Minor Negative
>
> To show a weak hand when opener shows a strong unbalanced hand by opening 2♣ and then bidding a suit, responder bids:
>
> * 3NT if opener bids 3♦.
> * 3♦ if opener bids 3♣.
> * 3♣ if opener bids 2♥ or 2♠.

This agreement is referred to as *cheaper minor negative*, since responder bids the cheaper available minor suit to show a weak hand, except after a 3♦ rebid by opener, when responder bids 3NT instead of 4♣. There are other possible agreements[36], but this is a popular approach.

If opener rebids the same suit after responder has shown a very weak hand, responder can then pass. This is the only way the partnership can stop below game when opener has a strong unbalanced hand.

Here are some examples of responder's rebid with a weak hand.

WEST	NORTH	EAST	SOUTH
		2♣	PASS
2♦	PASS	2♥	PASS
?			

♠ 9 8 3 2
♥ 6 5
♦ J 7 5 2
♣ 8 6 3

3♣. Your 2♦ response was an artificial waiting bid. Opener's 2♥ bid shows a strong hand of unlimited strength with a five-card or longer heart suit. Although you have a weak hand, you can't pass. The 2♥ rebid is forcing. Partner may have enough to make game even with no help from you. Your 3♣ bid is artificial and shows a weak hand. If partner now rebids the same suit, 3♥, you can pass. If partner rebids anything else, you'll have to keep bidding until game is reached.

---

[36] For example, some partnerships prefer to use 2NT as the weak response after a 2♥ or 2♠ rebid by opener and 3NT as the weak response after a 3♣ or 3♦ rebid by opener.

	WEST	NORTH	EAST	SOUTH
			2♣	PASS
	2♦	PASS	3♣	PASS
	?			

♠ 8 5 2
♥ J 8 6 3
♦ J 7 4
♣ 9 7 3

3♦. After East's 3♣ bid, responder bids the cheaper minor, 3♦, to show a weak hand. The advantage of this additional artificiality is that it leaves room for opener to now bid 3NT and play notrump from the stronger side, keeping East's cards hidden from the defenders.

There is one other weak action responder can take. With a fit for opener's suit but no other useful feature in a side suit, such as an ace, king, void, or singleton, responder can raise directly to game.

	WEST	NORTH	EAST	SOUTH
			2♣	PASS
	2♦	PASS	2♥	PASS
	?			

♠ 8 3
♥ Q 7 4 3
♦ 10 8 4 2
♣ 7 6 2

4♥. You only have 2 high-card points plus 1 dummy point for the doubleton spade. With four-card support for partner's suit, however, there should be a good chance for game. A raise directly to game is actually weaker than a raise to 3♥. It shows good trump support, but nothing else that is likely to be of use in case partner is thinking about going to the slam level.

WHEN RESPONDER HAS ABOUT 4 OR MORE POINTS

With about 4 or more points, responder should keep bidding until game is reached. Responder can raise with three-card or longer support, bid a five-card or longer suit, or bid notrump. For example:

WEST	NORTH	EAST	SOUTH
		2♣	PASS
2♦	PASS	2♥	PASS
?			

♠ 8 4
♥ Q 7 5
♦ K 7 6 2
♣ 10 9 6 5

3♥. With three-card support and 5 high-card points, you can raise partner's suit. The partnership is headed for at least a game contract in hearts, but you want to leave room in case opener has bigger things in mind, perhaps a slam contract. The raise to the three level is actually stronger than a jump raise to the four level, which would show no useful help outside the trump suit.

WEST	NORTH	EAST	SOUTH
		2♣	PASS
2♦	PASS	2♥	PASS
?			

♠ Q 10 7 6 5
♥ 6 2
♦ Q J 7 4
♣ 9 5

2♠. You don't have support for partner's suit but can show a five-card suit of your own. Partner won't expect too much. With a good five-card suit and 8 or more points, you would have made a positive response of 2♠ over 2♣.

WEST	NORTH	EAST	SOUTH
		2♣	PASS
2♦	PASS	2♥	PASS
?			

♠ Q J 5
♥ 10 4
♦ J 10 7 3
♣ Q J 9 3

2NT. You don't have support for partner's suit or a five-card or longer suit of your own. You do have a little something, however, and can suggest playing in notrump.

When Opener Rebids in Notrump

When opener rebids in notrump after the 2♦ waiting bid, responder can pass with a weak balanced hand. Opener's hand is no longer unlimited in strength. A 2NT rebid shows 22–24 points and a jump to 3NT shows 25–27 points.

After a 2NT rebid by opener, responder can use the Stayman convention and Jacoby transfer bids[37] in a manner similar to that after a 1NT opening bid:

Stayman and Transfers after Opener's 2NT Rebid

- 3♥ is a transfer, asking opener to bid 3♠.
- 3♦ is a transfer, asking opener to bid 3♥.
- 3♣ is Stayman, asking if opener has a four-card major suit.

With no interest in a major suit, responder can pass with about 0–2 points or raise to game with about 3–8 points[38].

For example, suppose you are West. Partner opens 2♣ and you respond 2♦. Partner now rebids 2NT and you have to decide what to do.

WEST	NORTH	EAST	SOUTH
		2♣	PASS
2♦	PASS	2NT	PASS
?			

♠ J 7 5
♥ 10 8
♦ 9 7 5 4 2
♣ 8 6 5

Pass. Your 1 high-card point and weak five-card suit are unlikely to be enough help for partner to take nine tricks, even though partner has 22–24 points.

---

[37] If the partnership uses Stayman but not transfer bids, responses of 3♦, 3♥, and 3♠ are natural, forcing bids, showing a five-card or longer suit.

[38] With about 9 or more points, responder can consider getting to slam. See Chapter 4.

WEST	NORTH	EAST	SOUTH
		2♣	PASS
2♦	PASS	2NT	PASS
?			

♠ 8 6
♥ J 6 4
♦ K 7 43
♣ J 9 7 2

3NT. With 5 high-card points and a balanced hand, take partner to game in notrump.

WEST	NORTH	EAST	SOUTH
		2♣	PASS
2♦	PASS	2NT	PASS
?			

♠ Q 8 6 3
♥ J 10 7 2
♦ 8 4
♣ Q 6 2

3♣. This is the Stayman convention—similar to a 2♣ response to an opening 1NT bid. If opener bids 3♥ or 3♠, showing a four-card major suit, raise to game. If opener bids 3♦, denying a four-card major, bid 3NT.

WEST	NORTH	EAST	SOUTH
		2♣	PASS
2♦	PASS	2NT	PASS
?			

♠ J 8 3
♥ Q 7 6 5 2
♦ Q 7 2
♣ 9 4

3♦. This is a transfer, asking opener to bid 3♥. You plan to then bid 3NT, giving opener the choice of playing game in notrump with only two hearts or bidding to 4♥ with three-card or longer support for hearts.

	WEST	NORTH	EAST	SOUTH
			2♣	PASS
	2♦	PASS	2NT	PASS
	?			

♠ Q 10 7 6 4 3
♥ 5
♦ K 7 2
♣ 9 8 3

3♥. This is a transfer, asking opener to bid 3♠. You will then raise to 4♠. You could simply jump to 4♠, but the contract would then be played from the weaker hand, with the stronger hand on the table as dummy. (See also Texas transfers in Appendix 2).

The partnership can also use Stayman and transfers after a 3NT rebid by opener:

Stayman and Transfers after Opener's 3NT Rebid

- 4♥ is a transfer, asking opener to bid 4♠.
- 4♦ is a transfer, asking opener to bid 4♥.
- 4♣ is Stayman, asking if opener has a four-card major suit.

	WEST	NORTH	EAST	SOUTH
			2♣	PASS
	2♦	PASS	3NT	PASS
	?			

♠ 4 2
♥ 10 8 6 5 3 2
♦ 4
♣ J 8 6 5

4♦. This is a transfer asking opener to bid 4♥. Even though you have a weak hand, 4♥ is likely to be a better contract than 3NT.

WEST	NORTH	EAST	SOUTH
		2♣	PASS
2♦	PASS	3NT	PASS
?			

♠ Q 10 7 4 2
♥ 3
♦ J 9 6 4 2
♣ 7 5

4♥. This a transfer asking opener to bid 4♠. After the 3NT bid by opener, you don't have enough room to find out whether opener has a doubleton spade or three or more. You have to make your best guess. Your hand is more likely to be useful with spades as trumps even if opener has only two.

The 2NT Opening Bid

An opening bid of 2NT shows:

- 20–21 points
- A balanced hand

Here are two hands that would be opened 2NT:

♠ K Q
♥ A J 7 2
♦ A Q 10 5
♣ K J 9

2NT. This is a balanced hand with 20 high-card points.

♠ K Q J
♥ K J 4
♦ A Q
♣ A 10 8 7 5

2NT. There are 20 high-card points plus 1 length point for the five-card club suit. With a balanced hand, open 2NT. This is more descriptive than opening 1♣.

Responding to 2NT

The 2NT opening is not forcing. Responder can pass with a balanced hand of about 0–4 points. With about 5 or more points, responder should get the partnership to game. Responder can use both Stayman and transfers after 2NT.

WEST	NORTH	EAST	SOUTH
		2NT	PASS
?			

♠ 8 7 3
♥ J 4
♦ Q 7 6 3
♣ 9 8 5 2

Pass. With only 3 high-card points, the partnership is unlikely to have enough combined strength for a game contract.

WEST	NORTH	EAST	SOUTH
		2NT	PASS
?			

♠ 8 2
♥ 7 4
♦ K 9 7 2
♣ Q J 8 7 3

3NT. With 6 high-card points plus 1 length point for the five-card suit, there is enough combined strength to go for a game contract. With no interest in a major suit, 3NT is the most likely game contract.

WEST	NORTH	EAST	SOUTH
		2NT	PASS
?			

♠ 6 2
♥ 9 8 7 5 4 2
♦ 9 3
♣ J 6 2

3♦. This is a transfer to 3♥. With only 1 high-card point plus 2 points for length in the six-card heart suit, you can then pass, leaving the partnership in partscore with hearts as trumps.

WEST	NORTH	EAST	SOUTH
		2NT	PASS
?			

♠ Q J 7 3
♥ 9 4
♦ A 8 6 2
♣ 7 4 3

3♣. This is the Stayman convention, asking if opener has a four-card major. If opener bids 3♦ or 3♥, bid 3NT. If opener bids 3♠, raise to 4♠.

Opening Balanced Hands

Here is how to show a balanced hand of any strength:

- 12–14 points — Open one of a suit, planning to rebid notrump at the cheapest level.
- 15–17 points — Open 1NT.
- 18–19 points — Open one of a suit, planning to jump in notrump at the next opportunity.
- 20–21 points — Open 2NT.
- 22–24 points — Open 2♣, planning to rebid 2NT.
- 25–27 points — Open 2♣, planning to rebid 3NT.

SUMMARY

When the partnership uses weak two-bids, all strong hands of about 22 or more points are opened with a strong artificial 2♣ bid.

Responding to 2♣

With about 8 or more points, responder can make a positive response:

- 2♥, 2♠, 3♣, or 3♦ shows a good five-card or six-card or longer suit.
- 2NT shows a balanced hand.

A positive response commits the partnership to at least a game contract.

With fewer than 8 points or a hand unsuitable for a positive response, responder makes the artificial waiting response of 2♦.

Opener's Rebid with a Balanced Hand

With a balanced hand, opener rebids:

- 2NT   22–24 points
- 3NT   25–27 points
- 4NT   28–30 points

A balanced hand of 20–21 points is opened 2NT.

Both the Stayman convention and Jacoby transfer bids can be used by responder after a 2NT opening bid or a 2♣ opening followed by a 2NT or 3NT rebid.

Opener's Rebid with an Unbalanced Hand

With an unbalanced hand, opener rebids the longest suit or the higher-ranking of two five-card or six-card suits. This is forcing to game unless responder shows a very weak hand (see below).

Cheaper Minor Negative

After opener shows a strong unbalanced hand, responder can show a very weak hand (0–3 points) by bidding the cheaper available minor suit at the three level, or 3NT if opener bid 3♦. If opener then rebids the same suit, responder can pass.

Quiz – Part I

South is the dealer. What call would South make with the following hands?

WEST	NORTH	EAST	SOUTH
			?

a) ♠ A K J 10 8 7 4
   ♥ K Q
   ♦ A K 3
   ♣ 4

b) ♠ K 3
   ♥ A Q J 2
   ♦ K J 10 7
   ♣ A K J

c) ♠ 3
   ♥ A K J 10 5
   ♦ A K Q 9 2
   ♣ K 4

d) ♠ A Q J
   ♥ A K Q
   ♦ A Q 10 8 3
   ♣ K 7

e) ♠ A K
   ♥ K J 9 7 6 3
   ♦ A
   ♣ K 8 7 3

f) ♠ A Q 7
   ♥ K Q J 4
   ♦ J 3
   ♣ A Q J 5

North opens 2♣ and East passes. What call would South make with the following hands?

WEST	NORTH	EAST	SOUTH
	2♣	PASS	?

g) ♠ 9 8 7 3
   ♥ 7 5 4
   ♦ 8 2
   ♣ 8 7 5 3

h) ♠ 8 4
   ♥ K 10 7 6
   ♦ Q 8 4 2
   ♣ J 9 6

i) ♠ A Q J 7 5
   ♥ 9
   ♦ 8 6 3
   ♣ Q 8 4 2

j) ♠ 9 4
   ♥ Q 8 7 6 3
   ♦ K Q 9 7
   ♣ Q 6

k) ♠ Q J 5
   ♥ K 8
   ♦ J 10 6 4
   ♣ Q 9 7 2

l) ♠ 7 3
   ♥ 9 4
   ♦ A Q 10 7 3 2
   ♣ K 9 5

Answers to Quiz – Part I

a) 2♣. There are 20 high-card points plus 3 length points for the seven-card spade suit. That's too much to open 1♠. Start with an artificial strong 2♣, planning to show the spades on the rebid.

b) 2♣. This is a balanced hand with 22 high-card points. Open 2♣, planning to rebid 2NT to show a balanced 22–24 points.

c) 2♣. This hand has 20 high-card points plus 1 length point for each five-card suit. That brings the total to 22 points, enough to open 2♣, planning to show the hearts and then the diamonds if partner can't support hearts.

d) 2♣. The hand is balanced and has 25 high-card points plus 1 length point for the five-card diamond suit. Open 2♣, planning to rebid 3NT to show a balanced hand with 25–27 points.

e) 1♥. This hand has 18 high-card points plus 2 length points for the six-card suit. That's not quite enough to open 2♣. If partner doesn't have enough strength to respond to 1♥, the partnership is unlikely to have enough for a game contract.

f) 2NT. An opening bid of 2NT shows a balanced hand with 20–21 points. This hand has 20 high-card points.

g) 2♦. The 2♣ opening is forcing and the strength of partner's hand is unlimited. Make an artificial waiting response of 2♦.

h) 2♦. The 2♦ waiting response shows any hand unsuitable for an immediate positive response.

i) 2♠. With 9 high-card points plus a good five-card suit with two of the top three honors, this hand qualifies for a positive response.

j) 2♦. Although this hand has 9 high-card points, it is not balanced and the heart suit is not good enough for a positive response of 2♥. Start with a waiting bid of 2♦.

k) 2NT. A positive response of 2NT shows a balanced hand with 8 or more points.

l) 3♦. With 9 high-card points and a good six-card diamond suit, including two of the top three honors, this hand is enough for a positive response. 2♦ would be the artificial waiting response, so jump to 3♦ to show diamonds.

Quiz – Part II

South opens 2♣, West passes, and North responds 2♦, the waiting response. After East passes, what rebid would South make with each of the following hands?

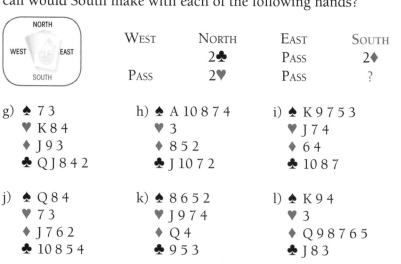

	WEST	NORTH	EAST	SOUTH
				2♣
	PASS	2♦	PASS	?

a) ♠ K 4
♥ A K Q J 9 7
♦ A K Q J
♣ Q

b) ♠ K Q 8 3
♥ A K 9 5
♦ A K 8
♣ K J

c) ♠ A Q 10 7 3
♥ A K Q J 4
♦ 5
♣ A Q

d) ♠ A K J
♥ A Q 8
♦ K 7
♣ A K J 10 4

e) ♠ K Q 7
♥ 4
♦ A K Q J 8 6 3
♣ A Q

f) ♠ A
♥ A K J 9 5
♦ 4
♣ A K Q 7 4 3

North opens 2♣, South responds 2♦, and North rebids 2♥. What call would South make with each of the following hands?

	WEST	NORTH	EAST	SOUTH
		2♣	PASS	2♦
	PASS	2♥	PASS	?

g) ♠ 7 3
♥ K 8 4
♦ J 9 3
♣ Q J 8 4 2

h) ♠ A 10 8 7 4
♥ 3
♦ 8 5 2
♣ J 10 7 2

i) ♠ K 9 7 5 3
♥ J 7 4
♦ 6 4
♣ 10 8 7

j) ♠ Q 8 4
♥ 7 3
♦ J 7 6 2
♣ 10 8 5 4

k) ♠ 8 6 5 2
♥ J 9 7 4
♦ Q 4
♣ 9 5 3

l) ♠ K 9 4
♥ 3
♦ Q 9 8 7 6 5
♣ J 8 3

Answers to Quiz – Part II

a) **2♥**. Time to show the nature of the 2♣ bid: a strong unbalanced hand with five or more hearts. There's no need to jump to game; 2♥ is forcing.

b) **2NT**. With a balanced hand and 23 high-card points, South rebids 2NT, promising 22–24 points. The 2NT rebid is limited and is not forcing.

c) **2♠**. With two five-card suits, start with the higher-ranking. This is similar to opening the bidding in the higher-ranking of two five-card suits.

d) **3NT**. Even with the five-card club suit, this is a balanced hand—no voids, no singletons, and only one doubleton. A jump rebid of 3NT shows a balanced hand with 25–27 points. This hand has 25 high-card points plus 1 point for the five-card club suit.

e) **3♦**. Partner's 2♦ response was artificial so this is the first natural bid. If the contract is played in diamonds, partner will be the declarer.

f) **3♣**. With more clubs than hearts, show the longer suit first. The hearts can be bid on the next round—and rebid to show five, if necessary.

g) **3♥**. Raise with support for partner's suit. There's no need to jump to game. Once a fit has been found, the partnership is committed to at least game.

h) **2♠**. With no fit for hearts, South can show the spade suit. Opener may have support for spades or be able to bid notrump knowing South has something in spades. Opener won't expect much since responder would have bid 2♠ right away with a good suit and 8 or more points.

i) **3♥**. Responder's priority is to raise opener's suit with support ahead of bidding a new suit.

j) **3♣**. With a very weak hand, no support for opener, and no suit to show, responder rebids the cheaper minor. This is totally artificial, warning opener that responder has about 0–3 points.

k) **4♥**. A jump raise of opener's major shows a weak hand with support for opener's suit and no side ace, king, void, or singleton.

l) **3♦**. With no fit for opener, responder can show the diamond suit. Opener won't expect a good suit since responder didn't make an immediate positive response.

Quiz – Part III

North opens 2♣, South responds 2♦ and North rebids 2NT. What call would South make with each of the following hands?

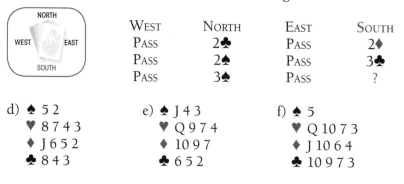

	WEST	NORTH	EAST	SOUTH
	PASS	2♣	PASS	2♦
	PASS	2NT	PASS	?

a) ♠ 8 3
♥ Q J 2
♦ Q 10 6 2
♣ 9 5 4 2

b) ♠ Q 9 8 6
♥ K 7 4 2
♦ 8 6 3
♣ 6 3

c) ♠ A 7 3
♥ J 9 8 6 4
♦ 6 4
♣ J 10 5

North opens 2♣, South responds 2♦, and North bids 2♠. South now bids 3♣ to show a weak hand and North rebids 3♠. What call would South make with each of the following hands?

	WEST	NORTH	EAST	SOUTH
	PASS	2♣	PASS	2♦
	PASS	2♠	PASS	3♣
	PASS	3♠	PASS	?

d) ♠ 5 2
♥ 8 7 4 3
♦ J 6 5 2
♣ 8 4 3

e) ♠ J 4 3
♥ Q 9 7 4
♦ 10 9 7
♣ 6 5 2

f) ♠ 5
♥ Q 10 7 3
♦ J 10 6 4
♣ 10 9 7 3

South opens 2♣ and North makes a positive response of 2♠. What call would South make with each of the following hands?

	WEST	NORTH	EAST	SOUTH
				2♣
	PASS	2♠	PASS	?

g) ♠ 3
♥ A Q J 8 7 5 3
♦ A K
♣ A Q 5

h) ♠ J 4
♥ A K Q
♦ A Q 10 5
♣ K Q J 6

i) ♠ K 10 7 3
♥ A 4
♦ A Q J
♣ A K J 3

Answers to Quiz – Part III

a) **3NT**. Opener's 2NT rebid shows 22–24 points. It is not forcing, but with 5 high-card points South has enough to raise to game.

b) **3♣**. Responder can use the Stayman convention, 3♣, after a 2NT rebid to look for an eight-card major suit fit. If opener bids 3♥ or 3♠, responder will raise to 4♥ or 4♠. If opener bids 3♦, responder will bid 3NT.

c) **3♦**. A 3♦ response to 2NT is a Jacoby transfer bid showing five or more hearts. After opener bids 3♥, responder can rebid 3NT to let opener choose between 3NT and 4♥.

d) **Pass**. Opener's rebid of the same suit after responder has shown a very weak hand is not forcing. It's time for responder to pass.

e) **4♠**. Responder doesn't have much, but there should be a chance that opener can make game opposite South's meager values.

f) **3NT**. Opener is going to have to take nine tricks to make 3♠. With responder's scattered values, it might be as easy to take nine tricks in notrump, which is a game contract.

g) **3♥**. North has made a positive response showing a good five-card or longer spade suit and 8 or more points. With no fit for spades, South simply bids the long suit. The partnership is committed to at least game.

h) **2NT**. With 22 high-card points but only two spades, South makes the rebid that best describes the hand. 2NT shows a balanced hand with 22–24 points.

i) **3♠**. South was planning to rebid 2NT, but with such excellent support for responder's suit can raise to show the fit. The partnership is committed to game and slam is a strong possibility. More on that in the next chapter.

DEAL: 9	♠ K 10 4
	♥ 9
DEALER: NORTH	♦ 10 9 8 6 2
VUL: NONE	♣ A 9 5 4

WEST		EAST
♠ J 8 6 5 3	NORTH	♠ A Q
♥ 10 7 3	WEST EAST	♥ A K Q J 8 4
♦ 7 5		♦ K Q J
♣ K 6 2	SOUTH	♣ 7 3

	SOUTH
	♠ 9 7 2
	♥ 6 5 2
	♦ A 4 3
	♣ Q J 10 8

Suggested Bidding

WEST	NORTH	EAST	SOUTH
	PASS	2♣	PASS
2♦	PASS	2♥	PASS
3♥	PASS	4♥	PASS
PASS	PASS		

North passes. East, with 22 high-card points plus 2 length points for the six-card heart suit, is too strong to open 1♥. Instead, East opens with an artificial forcing 2♣ bid. South passes.

West, with 4 high-card points plus 1 length point, would not have enough to respond if East had opened 1♥. However, East's 2♣ opening bid is forcing and West must bid something. West makes the artificial waiting response of 2♦.

East now shows an unbalanced hand with a five-card or longer heart suit by rebidding 2♥. There's no need to jump. The 2♥ rebid is forcing.

West can show the three-card support for hearts by raising to 3♥. Having found a fit, East can now put the partnership in a game contract of 4♥.

Suggested Opening Lead

South would lead the ♣Q, top of the solid sequence.

Declarer's Plan

Declarer starts by <u>A</u>ssessing the situation. East's goal is to take 10 tricks. The ♠A is a sure trick and there are six heart winners.

East next <u>B</u>rowses Declarer's Checklist. East can plan to promote two winners in the diamond suit. East can also hope to win a trick with either the ♣K or ♠Q with the help of a finesse. When <u>C</u>onsidering the Order, declarer might try winning a trick with the ♣K at trick one after South has led the ♣Q.

```
┌─ DECLARER'S PLAN—THE ABC'S ─┐
```

DECLARER'S PLAN—THE ABC'S

Declarer: East   Contract: 4♥

ASSESS THE SITUATION

Goal	10
Sure Tricks	7
Extra Tricks Needed	3

BROWSE DECLARER'S CHECKLIST

Promotion	2 in diamonds
Length	
The Finesse	1 in spades
	1 in clubs
Trumping in Dummy	

CONSIDER THE ORDER
- Draw trumps.
- Be in the right place at the right time to lead toward the ♠Q.

Unfortunately, this finesse doesn't work since North holds the ♣A[39].

With the ♣K trapped, the defenders can take the first two club tricks and may lead a third round which declarer can trump. Declarer's priority is to draw trumps and declarer can start by playing the ♥A-K. To try the spade finesse, declarer needs to lead from the West hand. So, when drawing South's remaining trump, declarer should lead a low heart to dummy's ♥10. Now declarer can lead a low spade from dummy. After North plays a low spade, declarer finesses the ♠Q. Since North holds the ♠K, the finesse works. Now declarer can drive out the ♦A to promote two diamond winners.

Comments

If East were to open 1♥, West might pass with fewer than 6 points and the partnership would miss the game contract. By opening 2♣ and rebidding 2♥, East is able to show a hand of about 22 or more points with a good heart suit and the partnership is able to reach 4♥.

---

[39] South is unlikely to hold the ♣A since a defender rarely leads away from an ace on opening lead against a suit contract. Expecting this, declarer might choose not to play dummy's ♣K.

DEAL: 10

DEALER: EAST
VUL: N-S

NORTH
♠ A K Q J
♥ K Q J
♦ Q 10 5
♣ A J 6

WEST
♠ 10 9 8 7
♥ 10 5
♦ A 9 7 3
♣ K Q 2

EAST
♠ 5 2
♥ A 9 7 4 3
♦ K 8 6
♣ 10 8 4

SOUTH
♠ 6 4 3
♥ 8 6 2
♦ J 4 2
♣ 9 7 5 3

Suggested Bidding

WEST	NORTH	EAST	SOUTH
		Pass	Pass
Pass	2♣	Pass	2♦
Pass	2NT	Pass	Pass
Pass			

East, South, and West pass. North has a balanced hand with 23 high-card points, too strong to open 2NT. North opens with an artificial forcing 2♣ bid. East passes.

Although South has only 1 point, South cannot pass the 2♣ opening bid. South makes the artificial waiting response of 2♦.

North can now make the descriptive rebid of 2NT, showing a balanced hand with 22–24 points. This is not forcing since North has now limited the hand to at most 24 points.

With only 1 point, South can pass. It is more likely that North holds 22 or 23 points than 24, so the partnership is unlikely to belong in a game contract. Even if North has 24 points, South's hand will probably not provide enough help for game.

Suggested Opening Lead

Against 2NT, East leads from the longest suit. With no sequence, East leads the ♥4, fourth highest.

Declarer's Plan

After the dummy comes down, North makes a plan. North's goal is to take at least eight tricks to make the 2NT contract. North counts the winners: four spades and the ♣A. Three more tricks are required.

Moving to the second stage, North browses Declarer's Checklist. The heart suit can provide two extra tricks through promotion. The defenders

DECLARER'S PLAN—THE ABC'S	
Declarer: North Contract: 2NT	
ASSESS THE SITUATION	
Goal	8
Sure Tricks	5
Extra Tricks Needed	3
BROWSE DECLARER'S CHECKLIST	
Promotion	2 in hearts
	1 in diamonds
Length	
The Finesse	
CONSIDER THE ORDER	
• Take the losses early in diamonds.	

have already led a heart, so the two heart winners are likely to be promoted as a matter of course. The North-South hands hold the ♦Q, ♦J, and ♦10, so the third extra trick can be promoted in the diamond suit by driving out the ♦A and ♦K. Since the lead must be given up twice to promote a diamond trick, declarer should develop that suit right away while keeping winners in the other suits to help regain the lead.

After winning the first heart trick, declarer can lead a diamond, for example, a low diamond to dummy's ♦J. Suppose West wins the ♦A and leads another heart, the best defense. East can win the ♥A and lead a third round of hearts to develop two more winners in the suit through length. Declarer wins the third round of hearts and leads the ♦Q, or ♦10. East can win the ♦K and take the two established heart winners, on which North discards two clubs, but declarer then has the remaining tricks.

Comments

By using the artificial 2♣ opening, North can describe a balanced hand too strong to open 2NT. A 2NT rebid is not forcing since it puts an upper limit on the strength of the hand. On this deal, it allows the partnership to stop in the best contract.

	♠ 8 6
	♥ A Q
	♦ A K Q J 10 7 6
	♣ A 5

DEAL: 11

DEALER: SOUTH
VUL: E-W

♠ A 5 4 2	NORTH	♠ Q J 10 9 3
♥ 10 9 8 7 6	WEST ⬥ EAST	♥ K 3
♦ 9 2		♦ 8 4
♣ K 9	SOUTH	♣ Q 8 4 2

	♠ K 7
	♥ J 5 4 2
	♦ 5 3
	♣ J 10 7 6 3

Suggested Bidding

WEST	NORTH	EAST	SOUTH
			PASS
PASS	2♣	PASS	2♦
PASS	3♦	PASS	3NT
PASS	PASS	PASS	

South and West pass. North has 20 high-card points plus 3 length points for the seven-card suit. That's enough to open with an artificial strong 2♣.

After East passes, South responds with an artificial waiting bid of 2♦. South has 5 high-card points plus 1 length point, not enough for a positive response.

North can now describe the nature of the hand by bidding 3♦ to show the long diamond suit. This is forcing, so South cannot pass. South doesn't have a strong enough or long enough suit to suggest another suit as trump, so South bids 3NT[40]. This should work well since South has some strength in each of the three *unbid* suits.

North, having described the hand, can now pass. 3NT appears to be the best contract since the North hand should provide at least nine tricks.

---

[40] South's 3NT bid could be made with a very weak hand since there is no 'cheaper minor' available at the three level after opener's 3♦ bid. However, North would pass anyway.

Suggested Opening Lead

Against 3NT, West leads the ♥10, top of the solid sequence in the longest suit.

Declarer's Plan

South's goal is to take at least nine tricks. The dummy can provide the nine winners: a heart, seven diamonds, and a club. With enough tricks to make the contract, all declarer has to do is take the tricks and run.

```
┌─ DECLARER'S PLAN—THE ABC'S ─┐
```

Declarer: South   Contract: 3NT

ASSESS THE SITUATION

Goal	9
Sure Tricks	9
Extra Tricks Needed	0

BROWSE DECLARER'S CHECKLIST

Promotion	
Length	
The Finesse	1 in hearts
	1 in spades

CONSIDER THE ORDER

- Take the tricks and run.

On the heart lead, South might be tempted to play dummy's ♥Q instead of the ♥A. The ♥Q will win the trick if West holds the ♥K. Even if East wins the ♥K, South's ♥J will now be promoted into a winner. South might also hope to take a trick with the ♠K if East holds the ♠A. However, South's priority is to make the contract.

The actual deal illustrates the danger if South doesn't win the first trick with the ♥A and take the first nine tricks. Suppose South tries the heart finesse by playing dummy's ♥Q. East will win the ♥K and may then lead the ♠Q. South's ♠K is then trapped and the defenders take five spade tricks to defeat the contract two tricks. Safety first!

Comments

After the 2♣ opening, the partnership reaches the best contract, as it turns out, from the best side. Even though the weaker hand is declarer, it works out best on this deal since the ♠K is protected. If West leads a spade, South will get a trick with the ♠K. If North were declarer in 3NT, East would lead the ♠Q and the defenders would take the first five tricks.

DEAL: 12
DEALER: WEST
VUL: BOTH

NORTH
♠ —
♥ J 9 5 4
♦ 10 8 7 4 2
♣ J 10 9 6

WEST
♠ A K Q 10 9 8
♥ A
♦ A K Q
♣ 7 5 3

EAST
♠ 7 5 4
♥ K Q 10 8 6
♦ J 3
♣ Q 8 4

SOUTH
♠ J 6 3 2
♥ 7 3 2
♦ 9 6 5
♣ A K 2

Suggested Bidding

WEST	NORTH	EAST	SOUTH
2♣	PASS	2♥	PASS
2♠	PASS	3♠	PASS
4♠	PASS	PASS	PASS

West has 22 high-card points plus 2 length points for the six-card spade suit. That's too much to open 1♠, so West starts with a strong artificial 2♣ opening.

North passes. East has 8 high-card points and a good five-card heart suit with two of the top three honors. That's enough to make a positive response of 2♥ to the 2♣ opening. The positive response commits the partnership to at least a game contract.

West doesn't have support for hearts, so West shows the strong spade suit. East has three-card support for spades and shows this by raising to the three level. Having found WHERE the partnership belongs, West can now continue to 4♠[41]. Having already made a positive response, East has nothing more to say.

Suggested Opening Lead

North makes the opening lead. North would lead the ♣J, top of the solid sequence.

---

[41] West might consider a slam contract (see next chapter).

Declarer's Plan

West is declarer and the goal is to take ten tricks. West can count three sure tricks in spades, three in hearts, and three in diamonds. However, declarer may not actually be able to take three heart tricks since there is no way to get to the dummy after taking the ♥A. As compensation, declarer can anticipate taking more than three tricks from the spade suit. With nine spades in the combined hands, declarer can expect to take six tricks from the suit if the missing spades are divided 2-2 or 3-1.

DECLARER'S PLAN—THE ABC'S

Declarer: West   Contract: 4♠

ASSESS THE SITUATION

Goal	10
Sure Tricks	9
Extra Tricks Needed	1

BROWSE DECLARER'S CHECKLIST

Promotion	
Length	2 or 3 in spades?
The Finesse	1 in spades
	1 in clubs
Trumping in Dummy	

CONSIDER THE ORDER

- Draw trumps.
- Be in the right place to lead toward the ♠10.

On the actual deal, the defenders can take the first three club tricks after the lead of the ♣J. So, declarer cannot afford to lose a spade trick. Suppose the defenders take the first three clubs and then lead a diamond. Declarer wins and leads the ♠A. North discards, revealing that South holds four spades, including the ♠J. To avoid losing a spade trick, declarer needs to take a finesse against South's ♠J. That requires leading a spade from dummy. To reach dummy, declarer should take a second diamond winner and then ruff the third diamond winner in dummy! Now declarer can lead the last spade from dummy and take a finesse against South's ♠J. Declarer draws the remaining trumps and loses only three club tricks, making the contract.

Comments

When a contract appears safe, declarer should guard against bad breaks in one or more of the key suits. On this deal, declarer has to play carefully to overcome the unexpected 4-0 break in the trump suit.

It may come as a revelation to many readers that defective, inferior, and unwarranted slam bidding is not a privilege reserved only for non-experts. It is inherent in all bridge players, and manifests itself wherever bridge players ply their trade. Somehow, however, one doesn't associate bad slam bidding with experts who, after all, appreciate full well that bidding is nothing more than a contractual estimate of the number of tricks one figures to win in the play. Nevertheless, overreaching oneself has become a dominant characteristic of most bridge players, at all levels.

—FRED KARPIN, HOW TO PLAY SLAM CONTRACTS (1961)

Slam Bidding

Most of the time, the partnership focuses on choosing between partscore and game: with about 25 or 26 or more points, the partnership goes for a game contract; with less combined strength, the partnership settles for partscore. Occasionally, however, the partnership has enough strength to take at least twelve tricks. Although this is rare, there are big *bonuses* for bidding and making a *small slam* contract, twelve tricks, or a *grand slam*, all thirteen tricks. So it is worthwhile to focus some attention on this exciting possibility.

Slam: How High?

To consider going for the slam bonus, the guideline is:

The Slam Zone	
Small Slam:	About 33 or more points
Grand Slam:	About 37 or more points

Notrump Contracts

For notrump contracts, it is often fairly straightforward to apply the guideline, especially when opener has accurately described the strength and distribution of the hand. Responder simply adds up the combined strength and decides whether to bid slam. For example:

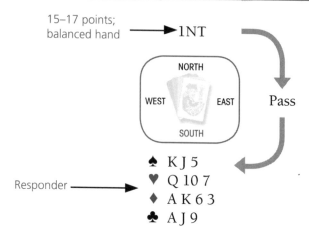

15–17 points; balanced hand ➤ 1NT

Pass

Responder ➤
♠ K J 5
♥ Q 10 7
♦ A K 6 3
♣ A J 9

6NT. Responder has 18 high-card points. Since the 1NT opening bid shows 15–17 points, responder knows the partnership has a minimum of 33 combined points (15 + 18) and a maximum of 35 combined points (17 + 18). That's enough for a small slam, but not a grand slam. Responder simply takes the partnership directly to the best spot.

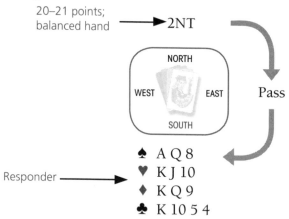

20–21 points; balanced hand ➤ 2NT

Pass

Responder ➤
♠ A Q 8
♥ K J 10
♦ K Q 9
♣ K 10 5 4

7NT. Here opener's 2NT bid shows a balanced hand with 20–21 points. Responder has 18 points. The partnership has a combined total of 38 (20 + 18) or 39 (21 + 18) points. That's enough to go for the grand slam bonus.

What if responder isn't sure whether there is enough combined strength for slam? Responder can make an invitational raise by bidding one level beyond game. This is often referred to as a *quantitative raise*, because the partnership is deciding on the level based purely on the quantity of high-card strength it holds.

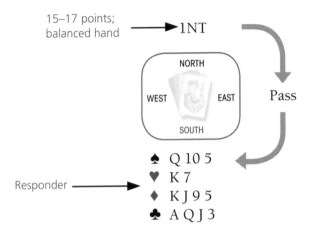

15–17 points; balanced hand ➤ 1NT

NORTH

WEST EAST · Pass

SOUTH

♠ Q 10 5
♥ K 7
♦ K J 9 5
♣ A Q J 3

Responder ➤

4NT. Opener is showing 15–17 points and responder has 16. If opener has 15 or 16 points, the combined strength is less than 33 points: 15 + 16 = 31; 16 + 16 = 32. If opener has a maximum, 17 points, then there is enough strength to go for slam: 17 + 16 = 33. So responder makes an invitational—quantitative—raise to 4NT, one level beyond the 3NT game contract. With a minimum, opener can pass and the partnership will stop in 4NT. With a maximum, opener can accept the invitation and continue to slam[42].

This is similar to raising 1NT to 2NT as an invitation to game. Opener can pass with a minimum to decline the invitation or can continue to game with a maximum.

---

[42] With 16 points, opener has neither a minimum nor a maximum. In general, opener declines an invitation with only 16 points but has the option of accepting, with a couple of extra 10's or 9s, perhaps. It's a judgment call.

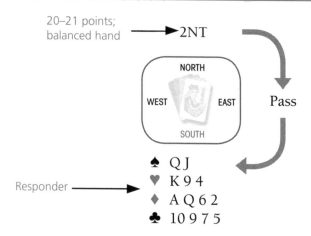

20–21 points;
balanced hand ⟶ 2NT

NORTH

WEST EAST

SOUTH

Pass

Responder ⟶

♠ Q J
♥ K 9 4
♦ A Q 6 2
♣ 10 9 7 5

4NT. The 2NT opening bid shows 20–21 points. Responder has 12. Responder invites slam by raising to 4NT. Opener will pass with a minimum, 20 points (20 + 12 = 32), and accept the invitation by bidding 6NT[43] with a maximum, 21 points (21 + 12 = 33).

The auction can sometimes take a little longer, but the general idea is the same. Suppose these are the combined partnership hands:

OPENER	RESPONDER
♠ K 6	♠ A Q 8 3
♥ A Q 5	♥ K 7 3
♦ K J 9 7 2	♦ Q 10 4
♣ K Q 4	♣ A 8 3

OPENER	RESPONDER
1♦	1♠
2NT	6NT
PASS	

Opener has 18 high-card points plus 1 length point for the five-card suit. That's too much to open 1NT, so opener starts with 1♦.

---

[43] Opener usually accepts by bidding 6NT but can sometimes look for a suit fit along the way by bidding a four-card suit at the five level or bidding a five-card suit at the six level.

Responder bids 1♠, and opener now shows the strength of the hand by jumping to 2NT, promising 18–19 points. Responder has 15 points and knows the partnership doesn't have an eight-card fit in spades, since opener didn't raise. Responder knows the partnership has either 33 (18 + 15) or 34 (19 + 15) combined points. That's enough information for responder to place the contract in 6NT.

OPENER	RESPONDER
♠ A K J	♠ Q 8 4
♥ Q J 5 2	♥ 10 7 3
♦ A Q J	♦ K 9 6 3 2
♣ A K 6	♣ J 8

OPENER	RESPONDER
2♣	2♦
3NT	4NT
PASS	

With 25 high-card points, opener starts with an artificial 2♣ and then jumps to 3NT over the 2♦ waiting response. With 6 high-card points plus 1 for the five-card diamond suit, responder knows the partnership is close to the slam zone since opener has shown 25–27 points. Responder invites a slam by raising to 4NT. With the bottom of the promised range, opener declines the invitation and the partnership stops in a game contract.

Suit Contracts

It is usually more challenging for the partnership to determine whether it belongs in the slam zone when a trump suit is involved. Opening bids, responses, and rebids in a suit often cover a wide range of strength. Also, hand valuation changes since the power of the trump suit brings voids and singletons into play.

Nonetheless, the partnership can sometimes bid slam in a trump suit on pure power. For example:

OPENER	RESPONDER
♠ A J 6 5	♠ K Q 10 7 3 2
♥ Q J 3	♥ A
♦ 9 5	♦ A J 7 3
♣ K Q 7 2	♣ A 8

OPENER	RESPONDER
1♣	1♠
2♠	6♠
PASS	

After the opening bid of 1♣, responder knows the partnership is in the slam zone. Responder has 18 high-card points plus 2 length points, for a total of 20. Since opener has at least 13, the partnership has 33 or more combined points. However, first things first. The partnership has to find a suitable trump fit. When responder bids 1♠ and opener raises to 2♠, responder knows where the partnership belongs. Also, the raise to 2♠ shows a minimum opening bid, so responder knows that a grand slam is unlikely. Responder can simply put the partnership in 6♠.

Responder has other options, as we shall see shortly, but this is a reasonable auction. With a little less strength, responder could bid 5♠, one level beyond game, inviting opener to bid 6♠ with more than a bare minimum.

Slam: WHERE?

The decision about WHERE to play a game contract is complicated by the scoring. Nine tricks are needed for game in notrump; ten tricks for game in a major suit; eleven tricks for game in a minor. The partnership doesn't always play in an eight-card or longer fit. When the fit is in a minor suit, 3NT is often a better choice since two fewer tricks are required.

The decision about WHERE to play a slam contract is more straightforward. Twelve tricks are required for a small slam in any denomination, a suit or notrump. The partnership typically chooses to play in a suit contract with an eight-card or longer fit; otherwise, in notrump.

The partnership's first priority is to look for a trump fit. Once the decision has been made about WHERE the contract should be played, the partnership can focus on HOW HIGH.

OPENER	RESPONDER
♠ K Q 7 6 5	♠ A 4
♥ Q 3	♥ A
♦ A J 4 3	♦ K Q 10 7 5
♣ 9 5	♣ A J 6 4 2

OPENER	RESPONDER
1♠	2♦
3♦	6♦
PASS	

Responder has 18 high-card points plus 2 length points. After the opening bid of 1♠, responder knows the partnership is in the slam zone (13 + 20 = 33). The first task, however, is to find a suitable trump suit. Responder starts with a response in a new suit. This is forcing. When opener raises, responder has found a fit. Opener's simple raise also shows a minimum opening bid, so responder decides the partnership belongs in a small slam and not a grand slam. So, responder knows both WHERE and HOW HIGH and can bid the slam[44].

The Blackwood Convention

Although the guideline of about 33 or more points for a small slam and 37 or more points for a grand slam works quite well for notrump contracts, there is an additional consideration in suit contracts. The partnership counts both length points and dummy points in

---

[44] Responder does have some other options as will be seen in the next section, but sometimes simple is best.

addition to high-card points. So the opponents may have enough high cards to take the first two tricks, especially since they have the advantage of the opening lead. Suppose these are the partnership hands:

OPENER	RESPONDER
♠ A Q J	♠ K 4
♥ Q 10 7 3	♥ K J 9 6 5 4
♦ 4	♦ A K Q J
♣ K Q J 10 8	♣ 9

OPENER	RESPONDER
1♣	1♥
3♥	6♥ ?
PASS	

After opener bids 1♣ and responder bids 1♥, opener revalues the hand. With four-card support for responder's hearts, opener can count 15 high-card points plus 3 dummy points for the singleton diamond, a total of 18. That's enough to make a jump raise to 3♥, showing a medium-strength hand of about 17–18 points. Responder has 17 high-card points plus 2 length points for the six-card heart suit, for a total of 19. Responder knows the partnership has at least 36 combined points (17 + 19) and could have 37 (18 + 19).

Even if responder takes a conservative view, however, and bids only a small slam, the contract is likely to be defeated. The defenders get to make the opening lead and can take the ♣A and the ♥A. Down one.

Note that the partnership does have lots of tricks. There are three spade tricks, five heart tricks after the ♥A is driven out, four diamond tricks, and four club tricks after the ♣A is driven out. That's a total of 16 tricks. The problem is that much of this strength is redundant. There are only 13 tricks that can be taken on any given deal, and if the defenders take the first two, it no longer matters how many tricks declarer can develop later.

Notice also that a contract of 6♥ isn't hopeless. If the defenders don't take their ♣A right away declarer can take three spade winners and discard the ♣9. Now the defenders will get only the ♥A. However, the partnership wants to avoid getting to a slam where the defenders could take the first two tricks. A grand slam of 7♥ would have no chance. The defenders are always getting a trick with the ace of the trump suit!

A critical ingredient in slam bidding is that the partnership must have enough aces so the defenders cannot immediately take the first two tricks. Aces are sometimes referred to as *first round controls*, since they control which side can win the first round of the suit. The reason the word 'control' is used is that a void can also serve as a first round control in a trump contract. If one partner is void in a side suit, declarer can trump the ace in that suit if the defenders lead it.

Kings are also important in slam bidding since they are *second round controls*, capable of winning the second round of the suit. In a trump contract, a singleton is a second round control since it prevents the defenders from taking more than one trick in the suit before declarer can trump.

So the partnership needs to make sure it has enough controls to bid a slam. To bid a small slam, the partnership needs first round control of three of the suits and at least second round control of the fourth. In other words, it can't be missing more than one ace. To bid a grand slam, the partnership needs first round control in all of the suits.

Recognizing this issue, Easley Blackwood in the early 1930s came up with a method of determining the number of aces held by the partnership. Although Easley's idea was at first ignored by the bridge authorities of the day, the Blackwood convention has become the most popular and well-known of all bridge conventions.

The Blackwood convention is used after the partnership has agreed on a trump suit. Then, a bid of 4NT asks how many aces partner holds. The replies are as follows:

Replies to Blackwood 4NT

↑ 5♠ Three aces
   5♥ Two aces
   5♦ One ace
   5♣ Zero or all four aces[45]

The 4NT bidder can then add up the number of aces held by the partnership to decide whether there are enough to bid a slam contract.

Let's see how it would help on our previous two hands:

OPENER	RESPONDER
♠ A Q J	♠ K 4
♥ Q 10 7 3	♥ K J 9 6 5 4
♦ 4	♦ A K Q J
♣ K Q J 10 8	♣ 9

OPENER	RESPONDER
1♣	1♥
3♥	4NT
5♦	5♥
PASS	

After the partnership has agreed on hearts as the trump suit and responder decides that the partnership has enough combined strength to belong in the slam zone, responder uses the Blackwood convention, 4NT, to ask for aces. Opener replies 5♦, showing one ace. Since responder has only one ace, the partnership has a total of two, leaving two for the defenders. Now responder knows that a small slam is not a good idea and stops in 5♥. Opener respects responder's decision.

---

[45] The 5 reply serves a dual purpose to leave 5NT available to ask for kings. The 4NT bidder can almost always determine whether the reply shows 0 or 4 since there is a 16 point difference.

Suppose we change opener's hand a little:

OPENER	RESPONDER
♠ A Q J	♠ K 4
♥ Q 10 7 3	♥ K J 9 6 5 4
♦ 4	♦ A K Q J
♣ A Q 10 8 2	♣ 9

OPENER	RESPONDER
1♣	1♥
3♥	4NT
5♥	6♥
PASS	

The auction would begin the same way, but now opener would reply 5♥ to the Blackwood convention, showing two aces. Responder would know only one ace is missing and could safely put the partnership in a small slam. The only trick lost would be the ♥A.

Suppose we make another change to opener's hand:

OPENER	RESPONDER
♠ A 7 5	♠ K 4
♥ A Q 10 7	♥ K J 9 6 5 4
♦ 4	♦ A K Q J
♣ A 10 8 6 2	♣ 9

OPENER	RESPONDER
1♣	1♥
3♥	4NT
5♠	7♥
PASS	

Again the auction starts the same way, but this time opener replies 5♠ to the Blackwood convention, showing three aces. Responder now knows the partnership has all the aces and is virtually assured of taking all 13 tricks: two spades, six hearts, four diamonds, and a club. Responder puts the partnership in a grand slam.

When the partnership has all the aces and enough combined strength to consider a grand slam, 5NT can be used as an extension of the Blackwood convention to ask about kings. The replies are:

Replies to Blackwood 5NT

↑	6NT	Four kings
	6♠	Three kings
	6♥	Two kings
	6♦	One king
	6♣	Zero kings

Here is an example of the use of Blackwood 5NT in an auction that involves a number of conventional bids:

OPENER	RESPONDER
♠ A K Q 8 6 5	♠ 10 7 4 2
♥ K Q 10 4	♥ A 5
♦ A Q	♦ 7 6 4
♣ A	♣ K 7 6 2

OPENER	RESPONDER
2♣	2♦
2♠	3♠
4NT	5♦
5NT	6♦
7♠	PASS

Opener begins with a strong artificial 2♣ and responder makes the 2♦ waiting response. Opener now shows the nature of the hand by bidding 2♠. With good support for spades and some values, responder raises to the three level. Opener can visualize a slam contract if the partnership has enough controls—aces and kings.

Opener bids 4NT, the Blackwood convention, to ask about aces. Responder's 5♦ reply shows one ace. Opener now knows the partnership holds all the aces and that there is the possibility of a grand slam if responder has one of the missing kings. Opener bids 5NT to ask about the number of kings held by responder. The 6♦ reply shows one. Opener doesn't care if it is the ♦K or the ♣K. If it is the ♦K, the partnership won't lose a trick in diamonds; if it is the ♣K, the ♦Q can be discarded on the ♣K. So, opener bids the grand slam. After trumps are drawn, opener's potential loser in the heart suit can be trumped in dummy.

When Blackwood Doesn't Work

Many players use the Blackwood convention whenever there is the possibility of a slam, but that is not the purpose of the convention. Blackwood was designed to keep the partnership out of poor slams rather than to get the partnership to good slams. The partnership must first determine that it has a suitable trump fit and enough combined strength to belong in the slam zone. Even then, Blackwood is only useful in determining the number of aces the partnership holds, not which aces. It is not suitable for every situation. Consider these hands.

OPENER	RESPONDER
♠ —	♠ A K 8
♥ A K 10 7 6 3	♥ Q J 5 2
♦ K Q J	♦ 10 8 7 6
♣ K Q J 4	♣ 3 2

OPENER	RESPONDER
1♥	3♥
?	

After responder makes an invitational jump raise showing four-card support for hearts and about 11–12 points, opener can visualize that the partnership could belong in the slam zone. If responder holds either the ♦A or ♣A, the partnership should be able to make 6♥. If responder has both the ♦A and ♣A, the partnership can probably make a grand slam[46].

However, the Blackwood convention is unlikely to help in this situation. In reply to 4NT, responder would show one ace, but opener would not know which ace. If opener bid 6♥, the defenders would take two tricks with the ♦A and ♣A.

Blackwood is not usually effective when holding a void[47]. A full discussion of handling such hands is outside the scope of this book, but it is of interest to know that there is an alternative. The partnership can use *cuebidding*. Cuebidding is an advanced topic, but the basic idea is that instead of asking about controls, you can show a specific control you have, such as an ace or a void, and partner can cooperate by showing a control.

For example, an advanced partnership might bid the hands this way:

OPENER	RESPONDER
1♥	3♥
3♠	4♥
PASS	

---

[46] Even though opener is missing the ♥Q, the partnership has at least 10 combined trumps. If responder doesn't hold the ♥Q, the three missing hearts are likely to divide 2-1.

[47] Or when holding two or more low cards in an unbid suit where the defenders might hold both the ace and king.

After the heart suit has been agreed, opener cuebids to show first round control of spades—a void in this case. Responder can now infer that the ♠A and ♠K are unlikely to be useful cards. Both partners have first round control in the same suit. With no first round control in either clubs or diamonds, responder simply returns to the trump suit. Opener now knows that the partnership is missing both the ♣A and ♦A, and settles for game.

Let's change responder's hand:

	OPENER		RESPONDER
♠	—	♠	K 8 5
♥	A K 10 7 6 3	♥	Q J 5 2
♦	K Q J	♦	A 8 7 6
♣	K Q J 4	♣	3 2

OPENER	RESPONDER
1♥	3♥
3♠	4♦
6♥	PASS

After opener shows interest in slam by cuebidding the spade void, responder cooperates by showing the ♦A, and opener bids to the excellent small slam[48].

Cuebidding takes practice by the partnership. At this point, it is probably best to ignore these types of situations and just use your best judgment when bidding a slam. Most of the time, you should be okay if the partnership has a suitable trump fit and enough strength to belong in the slam zone.

---

[48] Cuebids are typically made 'up the line'—cheapest first. When responder bypasses clubs to bid 4 , opener can infer that the partnership is missing the ♣A.

The Gerber Convention

There is another situation when the Blackwood convention can't be used. After a natural notrump bid, a bid of 4NT is a quantitative, invitational, bid as discussed earlier in the chapter. No trump suit has been agreed. So how can you ask about aces after partner bids notrump?

In the late 1930's, John Gerber of Houston, Texas, proposed a solution. The Gerber convention uses a jump to 4♣ to ask for aces after a natural 1NT or 2NT bid. The replies follow a similar pattern to that of the Blackwood convention:

Replies to Gerber 4♣	
4NT	Three aces
4♠	Two aces
4♥	One ace
4♦	Zero or all four aces

As with the Blackwood convention, the first step doubles up to show either 0 or all 4 aces. That leaves 5♣ available to ask for the number of kings held when the partnership holds all the aces and is interested in reaching a grand slam:

Replies to Gerber 5♣	
6♣	Four kings
5NT	Three kings
5♠	Two kings
5♥	One king
5♦	Zero kings

After getting a reply to the 4♣ Gerber convention, any bid other than 5♣—which asks for kings—is a sign off bid, setting the contract. Here are examples of the Gerber convention:

OPENER	RESPONDER
♠ A 8	♠ K Q J 9 7 5 2
♥ K Q J 8	♥ 4
♦ J 9 6 2	♦ K Q 7
♣ K Q 9	♣ A 6

OPENER	RESPONDER
1NT	4♣
4♥	4♠
PASS	

Responder has 15 high-card points plus 3 length points for the seven-card spade suit, for a total of 18. Since opener is showing 15–17 points with the 1NT bid, responder knows the partnership is in the slam zone. There are somewhere between 33 (15 + 18) and 35 (17 + 18) combined points. Responder also knows WHERE the partnership belongs, spades. The only question is whether the partnership has enough aces.

A bid of 4NT would not be the Blackwood convention, since no suit has been agreed by the partnership. It would be an invitational bid, asking opener to pass with a minimum or continue to slam with a maximum. Instead, responder uses the 4♣, Gerber, convention to ask how many aces opener holds. Opener's 4♥ reply shows one ace. Responder now knows the partnership is missing two aces, so slam is not a good idea. Responder signs off by bidding 4♠, and opener respects responder's decision.

Let's change opener's hand a bit:

OPENER	RESPONDER
♠ A 8	♠ K Q J 9 7 5 2
♥ A J 8 7	♥ 4
♦ J 9 6 2	♦ K Q 7
♣ K Q 9	♣ A 6

OPENER	RESPONDER
1NT	4♣
4♠	6♠
PASS	

Opener actually has fewer high-card points than in the previous hand, but the 4♠ reply shows two aces. Responder knows the partnership is only missing one ace and bids to the small slam.

Let's make another change to opener's hand:

OPENER	RESPONDER
♠ A 8	♠ K Q J 9 7 5 2
♥ A J 8 7	♥ 4
♦ A 9 6 2	♦ K Q 7
♣ K 9 5	♣ A 6

OPENER	RESPONDER
1NT	4♣
4NT	5♣
5♥	7♠
PASS	

This time opener's 4NT reply shows three aces. Responder knows the partnership has all the aces and can imagine a grand slam if opener has a king. Responder bids 5♣ as the extension to the Gerber convention to ask how many kings opener holds. Opener's 5♥ reply shows one king and that's enough information for responder to bid a grand slam.

The partnership has seven spade tricks, a heart, three diamonds, and two clubs, for thirteen tricks. It wouldn't actually matter whether opener had the ♥K instead of the ♣K; the partnership would still have thirteen tricks. In fact, responder could confidently bid 7NT rather than 7♠.

Here's a more complex bidding conversation involving the Gerber convention:

Opener	Responder
♠ A J 6	♠ 5
♥ J 4	♥ A K Q 10 7 6
♦ A K J 5 4	♦ Q 7 3
♣ Q J 10	♣ K 4 2

Opener	Responder
1♦	1♥
2NT	4♣
4♠	6♥
Pass	

With 17 high-card points plus 1 length point for the five-card diamond suit, opener bids 1♦ and then jumps to 2NT over the 1♥ response, showing a balanced hand too strong to open 1NT, about 18–19 points. Holding 14 high-card points plus 2 length points for the six-card suit, responder now knows the partnership is in the slam zone. Responder also knows that there is at least an eight-card heart fit, since opener is showing a balanced hand.

Wanting to make sure the partnership has enough aces, responder uses the Gerber convention, since opener's last bid was a natural bid of 2NT. A bid of 4NT would not be Blackwood since, as far as opener knows, no trump suit has been agreed.

Opener's 4♠ reply to Gerber shows two aces, so responder knows the partnership is missing only one ace. Responder puts the partnership in a small slam contract of 6♥.

SUMMARY

There are large bonuses for bidding and making slam contracts. To consider going to a slam contract, the partnership needs about:

- 33 or more combined points for a small slam, twelve tricks.
- 37 or more combined points for a grand slam, all thirteen tricks.

At the slam level there is no difference in the number of tricks to be taken whether in a minor suit, a major, or notrump. So the partnership should consider playing in any eight-card or longer fit, or in notrump if there is no known fit.

If the partnership has a suitable fit and enough strength to be at the slam level, a final consideration is to make sure the defenders can't take the first two tricks against a small slam, or the first trick against a grand slam. If the partnership has agreed on a trump suit, the Blackwood convention, 4NT, can be used to discover how many aces—and perhaps kings—the partnership holds.

Replies to Blackwood 4NT	
5♠	Three aces
5♥	Two aces
5♦	One ace
5♣	Zero or all four aces

Replies to Blackwood 5NT	
6NT	Four kings
6♠	Three kings
6♥	Two kings
6♦	One king
6♣	Zero kings

The Gerber convention, 4♣, can be used to discover how many aces the partnership holds when the last bid was a natural 1NT or 2NT:

Replies to Gerber 4♣

↑ 4NT Three aces
4♠ Two aces
4♥ One ace
4♦ Zero or all four aces

Replies to Gerber 5♣

↑ 6♣ Four kings
5NT Three kings
5♠ Two kings
5♥ One king
5♦ Zero kings

Quiz – Part I

North opens 1NT. What call would South make with the following hands?

WEST	NORTH	EAST	SOUTH
	1NT	PASS	?

a) ♠ K 8 5
   ♥ Q J 7
   ♦ K 9 6 3
   ♣ A Q 5

b) ♠ 10 6 2
   ♥ K Q 8
   ♦ A Q 4
   ♣ A K 8 3

c) ♠ K J
   ♥ Q J 10
   ♦ A 9 6 3
   ♣ K Q 10 6

North opens 2NT. What call would South make with the following hands?

WEST	NORTH	EAST	SOUTH
	2NT	PASS	?

d) ♠ K 9 4
   ♥ A Q 10
   ♦ K Q J 5
   ♣ K 8 3

e) ♠ K J 5
   ♥ J 8 6
   ♦ Q J 8 7 3
   ♣ A J

f) ♠ Q 6 2
   ♥ J 4
   ♦ A Q 7 2
   ♣ K 10 6 3

North opens 1♦, East passes, and South responds 1♥. West passes and North raises to 2♥. HOW HIGH is the partnership headed when South holds each of the following hands?

WEST	NORTH	EAST	SOUTH
	1♦	PASS	1♥
PASS	2♥	PASS	?

g) ♠ A 4
   ♥ A J 8 7 3
   ♦ 10 8 3
   ♣ K J 5

h) ♠ A J 6 3
   ♥ A Q J 8 7 3
   ♦ —
   ♣ K Q J

i) ♠ A Q 6
   ♥ K Q 10 5 2
   ♦ Q 7
   ♣ K J 4

Answers to Quiz – Part I

a) **3NT.** South has 15 high-card points and opener has promised 15–17 points. The partnership has a combined total of between 30 (15 + 15) and 32 (15 + 17) points. That's enough for game but not slam.

b) **6NT.** This hand has 18 high-card points. The combined partnership total is between 33 (15 + 18) and 35 (17 + 18) points. That's enough to go for a small slam bonus. Take the partnership right to 6NT.

c) **4NT.** There are 16 high-card points in this hand, so the partnership has between 31 (15 + 16) and 33 (17 + 16) points. There might be enough combined strength for a slam, but only if opener has a maximum. Make an invitational, quantitative, raise to 4NT.

d) **7NT.** This hand has 18 high-card points. Partner's 2NT shows 20–21 points, so the partnership has at least 38 combined points (20 + 18). That's enough to go for a grand slam in notrump.

e) **6NT.** This hand has 13 high-card points plus 1 length point for the five-card diamond suit, for a total of 14. The partnership has either 34 (20 + 14) or 35 (21 + 14) combined points. That's enough for a small slam, but not a grand slam. With no known eight-card fit, take the partnership to 6NT.

f) **4NT.** South has 12 high-card points. If opener has 21, the partnership has a combined total of 33 (21 + 12), enough for a small slam. Invite partner to bid a slam with a maximum by raising to 4NT, one level beyond game. With only 20 points, opener can decline the invitation and settle for the game bonus.

g) **Game.** Opener's raise to 2♥ shows support for hearts and a minimum opening, about 13–16 points. South has 13 high-card points plus 1 length point for the five-card heart suit, for a total of 14. The partnership has enough strength for game, but not slam.

h) **Slam.** South has 18 high-card points plus 2 length points for the six-card heart suit, for a total of 20. Even if opener has a minimum of 13 points, there is enough combined strength to put the partnership in the slam zone. South could keep the auction simple by raising to 6♥.

i) **Maybe Slam.** South has 17 high-card points plus 1 length point, for a total of 18. There might be enough combined strength for slam if opener has more than a bare minimum. South could invite opener to continue to slam by raising to 5♥, one level beyond game.

Quiz – Part II

South opens 1♣ and North responds 1♠. South raises to 3♠, and North now jumps to 4NT. What call would South make with each of the following hands?

WEST	NORTH	EAST	SOUTH
			1♣
PASS	1♠	PASS	3♠
PASS	4NT	PASS	?

a) ♠ K Q J 2
♥ 7 4
♦ K Q
♣ K Q J 7 3

b) ♠ Q J 4 2
♥ K 10 7
♦ 5
♣ A K J 6 2

c) ♠ A 10 6 2
♥ A Q J 4
♦ 5
♣ Q J 7 3

d) ♠ A Q 8 5
♥ A Q
♦ 9 3
♣ A 9 7 4 2

e) ♠ A 10 6 3
♥ A 4
♦ A 5
♣ A 10 7 6 5

f) ♠ K 10 6 2
♥ —
♦ K J 4
♣ K Q J 7 5 3

North opens 1♠, South responds 2♦, and North raises to 3♦. South bids 4NT, Blackwood, and North replies 5♦. What is South's next call on these hands?

WEST	NORTH·	EAST	SOUTH
	1♠	PASS	2♦
PASS	3♦	PASS	4NT
PASS	5♦	PASS	?

g) ♠ K 4
♥ A
♦ K Q J 9 7 3
♣ K Q 7 2

h) ♠ 5
♥ K 6
♦ A K Q 7 6 2
♣ A K J 5

i) ♠ K 5
♥ A K
♦ A J 10 8 7 4 2
♣ A K

Answers to Quiz – Part II

a) 5♣. Since spades have been agreed as the trump suit, North's 4NT bid is the Blackwood convention, asking for the number of aces held by South. With no aces, South makes the artificial reply of 5♣.

b) 5♦. With one ace, South makes the artificial reply of 5♦.

c) 5♥. With two aces, South replies 5♥ to the Blackwood inquiry.

d) 5♠. The 5♠ reply shows three aces.

e) 5♣. With all four aces, South replies 5♣. The 5♣ reply to Blackwood shows either zero aces or all four. Hopefully partner will know which is the case, since there is a 16 point difference between no aces and four aces.

f) 5♣. With no aces, South replies 5♣ to Blackwood. Even though the heart void may have the same effect as an ace, Blackwood only asks about the number of aces. Voids are not included[49].

g) **Pass.** North's 5♦ reply to Blackwood shows one ace. South now knows that the partnership is missing two aces and must settle for a game contract. The defenders could take the first two tricks if South were to put the partnership in 6♦.

h) 6♦. North's 5♦ reply shows one ace and South holds two aces. Since the partnership is missing only one ace, South can bid a small slam contract of 6♦.

i) 5NT. North's reply shows one ace, so the partnership has all four. South has enough strength to consider a grand slam, so South can ask how many kings North holds by bidding 5NT. If North shows one king, by replying 6♦, South can bid a grand slam, knowing that it must be the ♦K. If North doesn't have the ♦K, South will settle for a small slam.

---

[49] There are methods to show a void when responding to the Blackwood convention, but they are beyond the scope of this book.

Quiz – Part III

South opens 1NT and North jumps to 4♣. What call would South make with each of the following hands?

	WEST	NORTH	EAST	SOUTH
				1NT
	PASS	4♣	PASS	?

a) ♠ K J 4
♥ K Q 7
♦ J 5
♣ K Q 10 8 5

b) ♠ A Q 7 3
♥ 10 3
♦ A J 5 2
♣ A 9 4

c) ♠ A 8 5
♥ A 10 7 3
♦ A 9 6 4
♣ A J

As South, you hold this hand:

♠ A 8 2
♥ K Q 7 4
♦ K 3
♣ K Q 5 4

What call do you make in each of the following auctions?

d)

WEST	NORTH	EAST	SOUTH
	1♦	PASS	1♥
PASS	3♥	PASS	?

e)

WEST	NORTH	EAST	SOUTH
			1NT
PASS	4NT	PASS	?

f)

WEST	NORTH	EAST	SOUTH
			1NT
PASS	4♣	PASS	?

g)

WEST	NORTH	EAST	SOUTH
			1NT
PASS	4♣	PASS	4♥
PASS	4NT	PASS	?

Answers to Quiz – Part III

a) 4♦. North's jump to 4♣ is the Gerber convention, asking how many aces South holds. With no aces, South replies with the cheapest step, 4♦. This has nothing to do with diamonds; it is a totally artificial reply, showing no aces.

b) **4NT**. With three aces, South replies 4NT to the Gerber convention. This has nothing to do with Blackwood or notrump. It is simply the artificial reply showing three aces.

c) 4♦. When replying to the Gerber convention, 4♦ shows either zero aces or all four aces. Presumably partner will know which case it is, since there is a 16-point difference.

d) **4NT**. North's opening bid followed by a jump raise of South's hearts shows four-card support and a medium-strength hand of about 17–18 points. South has 17 points, so the combined strength puts the partnership in the slam zone. South can make sure that the opponents don't have two aces to take by using the Blackwood convention. If partner replies 5♦, one ace, South will stop in 5♥. If partner shows two aces, 5♥, South can safely bid 6♥. If partner shows three aces, South might consider bidding 5NT to ask for kings and look for a grand slam…ambitious, but a reasonable gamble.

e) **6NT**. Partner's raise to 4NT is quantitative, inviting South to bid a slam. With a maximum, South can accept the invitation.

f) 4♥. Partner's jump to 4♣ is the Gerber convention, asking how many aces South holds. The 4♥ reply shows one.

g) **Pass**. North has used the Gerber convention and South has shown one ace. North's 4NT bid is now a signoff. Presumably, the partnership is missing at least two aces. South respects partner's decision to stop below slam.

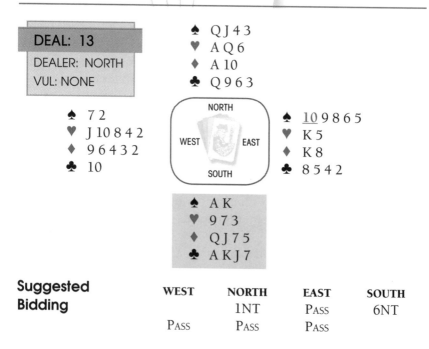

	♠	QJ43
	♥	AQ6
	♦	A10
	♣	Q963

DEAL: 13
DEALER: NORTH
VUL: NONE

West:
♠ 72
♥ J10842
♦ 96432
♣ 10

East:
♠ 109865
♥ K5
♦ K8
♣ 8542

South:
♠ AK
♥ 973
♦ QJ75
♣ AKJ7

Suggested Bidding

WEST	NORTH	EAST	SOUTH
	1NT	Pass	6NT
Pass	Pass	Pass	

North has a balanced hand with 15 high-card points and opens 1NT. East passes.

South has a balanced hand with 18 high-card points. South knows the partnership has at least 33 combined points (15 + 18) and at most 35 combined points (17 + 18). So South knows How High, small slam. With a balanced hand and no four-card or longer major suit, South also knows Where, notrump. Putting it together, South takes the partnership directly to a small slam in notrump, 6NT.

West passes. North has nothing further to say, since South has decided on the contract. East passes, and the auction is over.

Suggested Opening Lead

East would lead the ♠10, top of the solid sequence, against the small slam contract.

Declarer's Plan

A small slam is like any other contract, declarer starts by Assessing the situation. North's goal is to take 12 tricks. There are four sure spade tricks, a heart, a diamond, and four clubs. Declarer needs two more winners.

One possibility for an extra trick is the heart finesse. If West has the ♥K, declarer can lead a low heart from dummy and successfully finesse the ♥Q. This is only a 50-50 chance, and it would only provide one extra trick.

```
┌─ DECLARER'S PLAN—THE ABC'S ─┐

Declarer: North   Contract: 6NT

ASSESS THE SITUATION
  Goal                    12
  Sure Tricks             10
  Extra Tricks Needed    2

BROWSE DECLARER'S CHECKLIST
  Promotion        2 in diamonds
  Length
  The Finesse        1 in hearts
  Trumping in dummy

CONSIDER THE ORDER
  • With more than one choice,
    choose the alternative with the
    best chance.
  • Take the loss early in diamonds.
```

A better approach is to promote two extra winners in diamonds. This is sure to work, whichever defender holds the ♦K. South wins the first spade trick and plays the ♦5 to the ♦A and leads the ♦10, playing the ♦7 from dummy[50]. East wins the ♦K, but now both dummy's ♦Q and ♦J are winners. Whatever East leads next, declarer wins and takes the remaining tricks. North's ♥Q and ♥6 can be discarded on the diamond winners; there's no need to take the heart finesse.

Declarer must lose a trick to the ♦K early, while still retaining winners in all the other suits to regain the lead. If declarer were to take all the spade winners, for example, before playing diamonds, East would have a spade winner to take on winning the ♦K.

Comments

Once North opens 1NT, South can immediately place the contract in a small slam in notrump. The descriptiveness of the 1NT opening often makes it easy for responder to decide How HIGH and WHERE.

---

[50] Declarer could finesse the ♦10 instead of playing the ♦A followed by the ♦10. It won't make any difference on this deal. East will get a trick with the ♦K in either case.

DEAL: 14

DEALER: EAST
VUL: N-S

NORTH
♠ J 10 9 6 4
♥ 9 4
♦ 4 3
♣ 9 7 3 2

WEST
♠ A 5
♥ A Q J 8 3
♦ K 7
♣ K Q 8 6

EAST
♠ Q 7
♥ K 10 7 5
♦ A Q J 9 5
♣ J 4

SOUTH
♠ K 8 3 2
♥ 6 2
♦ 10 8 6 2
♣ A 10 5

Suggested Bidding

WEST	NORTH	EAST	SOUTH
		1♦	PASS
1♥	PASS	2♥	PASS
4NT	PASS	5♦	PASS
6♥	PASS	PASS	PASS

East has 13 high-card points plus 1 length point for the five-card diamond suit. East opens the long suit, 1♦. South passes.

West has 19 high-card points plus 1 length point for the five-card heart suit. That's a total of 20 points. West knows right away that the partnership is headed for the slam level, since there are at least 33 combined points (13 + 20). However, West doesn't know WHERE. West responds 1♥, looking for a fit. North passes.

With support for hearts and a minimum opening bid, East raises to 2♥. West now knows the partnership has a fit in hearts and enough combined strength for a slam. The final consideration is to make sure the partnership is not missing two aces. West uses the Blackwood convention, 4NT, to ask how many aces partner holds. East's 5♦ reply shows one ace, so West can confidently bid 6♥, knowing the partnership is missing only one ace.

Suggested Opening Lead

Against 6♥, North leads the ♠J, top of the solid sequence.

Declarer's Plan

West plans the play. West's goal is to take twelve tricks to make 6♥. There is a sure spade winner, five hearts, and four diamonds. Two more tricks are required.

West browses Declarer's Checklist. The diamond suit is likely to provide an extra trick through length, unless the missing diamonds divide very badly. Two tricks can be promoted in the club suit by driving out the ♣A, so declarer has plenty of tricks.

> **DECLARER'S PLAN—THE ABC'S**
>
> Declarer: West   Contract: 6♥
>
> **ASSESS THE SITUATION**
> | | |
> |---|---|
> | Goal | 12 |
> | Sure Tricks | 10 |
> | Extra Tricks Needed | 2 |
>
> **BROWSE DECLARER'S CHECKLIST**
> | | |
> |---|---|
> | Promotion | 2 in clubs |
> | Length | 1 diamonds |
> | The Finesse | |
> | Trumping in dummy | |
>
> **CONSIDER THE ORDER**
> - Draw trumps and then play diamonds, discarding the ♠5 from declarer's hand.

There is a danger, however. North's lead of the ♠J establishes a spade winner for the defenders. Declarer can try playing dummy's ♠Q on the first trick in case North holds the ♠K, but South plays the ♠K to drive out West's ♠A. If declarer draws trumps and then leads a club, the defenders can take two tricks: the ♣A and the established spade winner. To prevent this, declarer must make sure the defenders can't take a spade trick on winning the ♣A.

After winning the ♠A and drawing the defenders' trumps, declarer must first take the diamond winners, discarding the ♠5 on the third round of diamonds. Declarer can also discard two clubs. Now it is safe to drive out the ♣A. If the defenders lead a spade after winning the ♣A, declarer can trump and take the remaining tricks.

Comments

After the partnership has agreed on a trump suit and there is enough combined strength for a slam, the Blackwood convention can be used to make sure that the defenders cannot take too many immediate tricks to defeat the contract.

DEAL: 15	♠ 8 2
DEALER: SOUTH	♥ 10 8 5 3 2
VUL: E-W	♦ A 6 2
	♣ 9 5 3

```
            NORTH
♠ A J 10 6              ♠ K Q 9 7 5 3
♥ K Q        WEST EAST  ♥ A J 7
♦ Q J                   ♦ K 5 4
♣ K Q J 10 6            ♣ 8
            SOUTH
```

South hand:
♠ 4
♥ 9 6 4
♦ 10 9 8 7 3
♣ A 7 4 2

Suggested Bidding

WEST	NORTH	EAST	SOUTH
			PASS
1♣	PASS	1♠	PASS
4♠	PASS	4NT	PASS
5♦	PASS	5♠	PASS
PASS	PASS		

South passes. West has 19 high-card points plus 1 length point for the five-card club suit. With an unbalanced hand, two doubletons, West opens 1♣.

After North passes, East responds 1♠. South passes. With four-card support for spades and maximum-strength opening bid, West raises to 4♠, showing about 19–21 points.

East has 13 high-card points plus 2 length points for the six-card spade suit. After West raises spades, East knows WHERE the partnership belongs. East also knows that the partnership has enough combined strength for a slam, provided the defenders cannot take the first two tricks.

East uses the Blackwood convention to check for aces. West's 5♦ reply shows one. East now knows that the partnership is missing two aces, so 6♠ will not be a good contract. East signs off by bidding

5♠. West respects partner's decision and passes. The partnership stops short of slam.

Suggested Opening Lead

Against 5♠, South leads the ♦10, top of the solid sequence.

Declarer's Plan

East's goal is to take at least eleven tricks. There are six sure spade winners and three heart winners. Two more tricks are needed.

Two tricks can be promoted in the diamond suit. Three more tricks can be promoted in the club suit, and declarer can likely develop a fourth trick in that suit through length.

So declarer has plenty of tricks, which is why East was considering a slam. The problem on this deal is that the defenders can take two tricks before declarer can develop enough tricks to make a slam. After South leads the ♦10, North can win the ♦A. Later, South can take the ♣A to hold declarer to eleven tricks.

Declarer will have a surplus of winners after the ♦A and ♣A are driven out, but they will fall on one another. Declarer can't take more than eleven tricks after the defenders have already taken two tricks.

DECLARER'S PLAN—THE ABC'S

Declarer: East   Contract: 5♠

ASSESS THE SITUATION

Goal	11
Sure Tricks	9
Extra Tricks Needed	2

BROWSE DECLARER'S CHECKLIST

Promotion	2 in diamonds
	3 in clubs
Length	
The Finesse	
Trumping in dummy	

CONSIDER THE ORDER

- Draw trumps and then promote the club and diamond winners.

Comments

The challenge on this deal is to avoid reaching a slam which can easily be beaten by the defenders. The Blackwood convention is designed to keep the partnership out of bad slams, not to get the partnership to good slams.

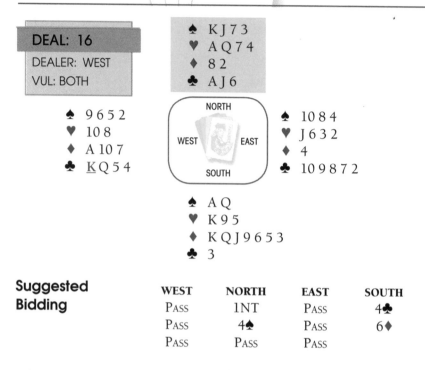

DEAL: 16		♠ K J 7 3	
DEALER: WEST		♥ A Q 7 4	
VUL: BOTH		♦ 8 2	
		♣ A J 6	

```
              NORTH
    ♠ 9 6 5 2                    ♠ 10 8 4
    ♥ 10 8      WEST   EAST      ♥ J 6 3 2
    ♦ A 10 7                     ♦ 4
    ♣ K Q 5 4                    ♣ 10 9 8 7 2
              SOUTH
```

♠ A Q
♥ K 9 5
♦ K Q J 9 6 5 3
♣ 3

Suggested Bidding

WEST	NORTH	EAST	SOUTH
Pass	1NT	Pass	4♣
Pass	4♠	Pass	6♦
Pass	Pass	Pass	

After West passes, North opens 1NT with 15 high-card points and a balanced hand. East passes.

South has 15 high-card points plus 3 length points for the seven-card diamond suit. That's a total of 18. Since North must have at least 15 points for the 1NT opening bid, South knows the partnership has at least 33 combined points. South knows the answer to How High, slam. South also knows Where, diamonds. The only question is whether the partnership is missing too many aces. To check on this, South uses the Gerber convention, 4♣. 4NT would not be the Blackwood convention since no suit has been agreed. It would be a quantitative raise, inviting opener to bid slam.

North's 4♠ reply shows two aces. South now knows the partnership is missing only one ace. That's okay for a small slam. South puts the partnership in 6♦.

Suggested Opening Lead

West makes the opening lead. Against 6♦, West would lead the ♣K, top of the touching high cards.

Declarer's Plan

South is declarer and the goal is to take twelve tricks. There are four sure tricks in spades, three in hearts, and one in clubs. Four more tricks need to be developed.

There is no difficulty in finding the extra tricks. Six tricks can be developed through promotion in the diamond suit. That's more than enough tricks. Declarer still won't be able to take all thirteen tricks, since

```
┌─ DECLARER'S PLAN—THE ABC'S ─┐
  Declarer: South    Contract: 6♦

  ASSESS THE SITUATION
    Goal                  12
    Sure Tricks            8
    Extra Tricks Needed    4

  BROWSE DECLARER'S CHECKLIST
    Promotion        6 in diamonds
    Length
    The Finesse
    Trumping in dummy

  CONSIDER THE ORDER
    • Take the loss early in diamonds.
    • Draw trumps.
```

one trick must be lost to the defender's ♦A.

After winning the ♣A, declarer's first task is to draw trumps. If declarer were to try to take the three heart winners first, for example, West would trump the third round with the ♦7 and the defenders would get two diamond tricks. So, declarer leads a high diamond to drive out the ♦A. Whatever the defenders lead next, declarer wins and draws the remaining trumps. Once that is done, declarer can safely take the rest of the tricks.

Comments

After a natural opening bid of 1NT or 2NT, the Gerber convention is used to ask about aces. On this deal, South can determine that the partnership is missing only one ace and put the partnership in the excellent small slam contract of 6♦[51].

---

[51] South might be tempted to bid 6NT instead of 6♦. However, 6NT can be defeated if West leads the ♣K. On winning the ♦A, West can take the ♣Q. 6♦ is a much safer contract.

Practice, the master of all things.

—Augustus Octavius, First Century B.C.

Additional Practice Deals

DEAL: 17

DEALER: NORTH
VUL: NONE

♠ Q 7 2
♥ 10 5 4 3
♦ K 10 7 4
♣ 10 9

```
              NORTH
♠ A 9 4                      ♠ J 6 3
♥ K Q 9    WEST     EAST     ♥ A J 7
♦ 8 6 3                      ♦ A Q J 5
♣ A K 5 4                    ♣ Q 6 3
              SOUTH
```

♠ K 10 8 5
♥ 8 6 2
♦ 9 2
♣ J 8 7 2

Suggested Bidding

WEST	NORTH	EAST	SOUTH
	PASS	1NT	PASS
4NT	PASS	PASS	PASS

North passes. With a balanced hand and 15 high-card points, East opens 1NT. South passes.

With a balanced hand and no four-card or longer major suit, West has the answer to WHERE, notrump. The only question is HOW HIGH: game or slam? Approximately 33 combined points are needed for a small slam. West has 16 high-card points. If East has 15 or 16 points, there won't be enough for slam; if East has 17 points, the partnership will have 33 points, enough to go for the slam bonus. To invite partner to slam, West makes a quantitative raise to 4NT.

With a minimum for the 1NT opening bid, East declines the invitation by passing. The partnership stops below the slam level in a contract of 4NT.

Suggested Opening Lead

South chooses the longest and strongest suit to lead, spades. With no sequence, South would lead the fourth highest, the ♠5.

Declarer's Plan

Declarer starts by <u>A</u>ssessing the situation. East's goal is to take 10 tricks. There is one spade winner, three heart winners, a diamond winner, and three club winners. That's a total of eight. Two more tricks are needed.

East moves to the second planning stage and <u>B</u>rowses Declarer's Checklist. East could hope for an extra trick through

```
┌─ DECLARER'S PLAN—THE ABC'S ─┐
Declarer: East    Contract: 4NT

ASSESS THE SITUATION
  Goal                     10
  Sure Tricks               8
  Extra Tricks Needed   2

BROWSE DECLARER'S CHECKLIST
  Promotion
  Length
  The Finesse          2 in diamonds

CONSIDER THE ORDER
  • Use the entries to dummy to take
    repeated diamond finesses.
└─────────────────────────────┘
```

length from the club suit, but that is against the odds. An even number of missing cards tends to divide slightly unevenly. So, the six missing clubs are more likely to be divided 4-2 than 3-3. A better source of tricks is the diamond suit. Diamonds could provide two extra tricks with the help of the finesse, if North holds the ♦K.

To take repeated diamond finesses, declarer needs entries to the West hand. In <u>C</u>onsidering the Order, declarer should make sure to lead diamonds when the lead is in the dummy. After winning a trick with the ♠A, declarer can lead a diamond and finesse the ♦J when North plays a low diamond. When the finesse is successful, declarer can get back to dummy with one of the heart winners and lead another low diamond and finesse the ♦Q. That gives declarer the two extra tricks needed to make the contract.

Comments

East-West do well to stop in a game contract and keep out of a slam, since they have only 31 combined points. On this deal, even a game contract is in some danger of being defeated if South held the ♦K instead of North. The quantitative raise lets the partnership explore the possibility of slam without getting too high when there is not enough combined strength.

DEAL: 18		♠ J 7
		♥ Q J 10 6
DEALER: EAST		♦ 10 7 3 2
VUL: N-S		♣ Q 7 3

♠ K 10 8 6 4	NORTH	♠ A 5 3 2
♥ 5 3		♥ K 8 4
♦ A 6	WEST EAST	♦ 9 5 4
♣ 10 9 8 4	SOUTH	♣ 6 5 2

♠ Q 9
♥ A 9 7 2
♦ K Q J 8
♣ A K J

Suggested Bidding

WEST	NORTH	EAST	SOUTH
		PASS	2NT
PASS	3♣	PASS	3♥
PASS	4♥	PASS	PASS
PASS			

East passes and South has a balanced hand with 20 high-card points. South opens 2NT, showing 20–21 points. West passes.

North has 6 high-card points, enough to get the partnership to a game contract. The only question is WHERE? To determine whether the partnership has an eight-card heart fit, North uses the Stayman convention, 3♣ in response to the opening bid of 2NT.

South shows the four-card heart suit in reply to the Stayman inquiry, and North puts the partnership in game in hearts, 4♥.

Suggested Opening Lead

West leads the ♣10, top of the solid three-card sequence in clubs, against the 4♥ contract. Leading from a solid sequence is usually preferable to leading low, away from an honor, against a suit contract.

Declarer's Plan

After North puts down the dummy, South makes a plan. South's goal is to take at least ten tricks. There is one sure heart trick and three sure club tricks. Six more tricks are required.

South browses Declarer's Checklist. Three tricks can be promoted in the diamond suit. In the heart suit, two more tricks could be promoted by simply driving out trumps. However, three extra tricks are needed. Three additional tricks can be taken in the heart suit

---

┌─ DECLARER'S PLAN—THE ABC'S ─┐

Declarer: South   Contract: 4♥

ASSESS THE SITUATION

Goal	10
Sure Tricks	4
Extra Tricks Needed	6

BROWSE DECLARER'S CHECKLIST

Promotion	3 in diamonds
Length	
The Finesse	3 in hearts
Trumping in dummy	

CONSIDER THE ORDER

- be in the right hand to lead hearts and trap the defender's ♥K.
- Draw trumps.
- Take the loss early in diamonds, after trumps are drawn.

---

with the help of the finesse. Declarer will have to hope that East holds the ♥K.

To trap East's ♥K, declarer needs to lead hearts from the dummy. So declarer wins the first trick with dummy's ♣Q. Then declarer leads dummy's ♥Q. Assuming East plays a low heart, South also plays a low heart. The finesse works, because West doesn't hold the ♥K. Declarer can repeat the finesse by leading the ♥J from dummy. If East plays a low heart, declarer plays a low heart from the South hand; if East plays the ♥K, it is captured by South's ♥A. By continuing with a third round of hearts, East's ♥K is captured and declarer has drawn all the defenders' trumps at the same time.

Once the trumps are drawn, declarer can safely lead diamonds to drive out the ♦A and promote three winners in the suit. South still has club winners and a trump winner with which to regain the lead.

Comments

North and South do well to play game in the eight-card heart fit rather than 3NT. Against 3NT, West would lead the ♣6, and the defenders can take the first five tricks. The Stayman convention lets North-South find the heart fit after the 2NT opening.

DEAL: 19	♠ 8 6 4
DEALER: SOUTH	♥ K 3
VUL: E-W	♦ K 10 4
	♣ Q J 10 6 3

♠ K 9 5   ♠ A 2
♥ Q 9 5   ♥ J 10 8 7 4 2
♦ A 9 8 6 5   ♦ Q 7 3
♣ A K   ♣ 8 5

♠ Q J 10 7 3
♥ A 6
♦ J 2
♣ 9 7 4 2

Suggested Bidding

WEST	NORTH	EAST	SOUTH
			PASS
1NT	PASS	2♦	PASS
2♥	PASS	3♥	PASS
4♥	PASS	PASS	PASS

South passes. West opens 1NT with a balanced hand of 16 high-card points plus 1 length point for the five-card diamond suit.

North passes. With a six-card heart suit, East knows WHERE the partnership belongs, hearts. East has 7 high-card points plus 2 length points for the six-card suit, for a total of 9. East is unsure HOW HIGH the partnership belongs since the partnership total is between 24 (15 + 9) and 26 (17 + 9). East wants to invite opener to continue to game with a maximum for the 1NT opening.

East starts by bidding 2♦, a Jacoby transfer bid, asking opener to bid 2♥. After West bids 2♥, East raises to 3♥, inviting opener to game in hearts. With 17 points, opener accepts the invitation and bids 4♥.

Suggested Opening Lead

North leads the ♣Q, top of the solid sequence, against the 4♥ contract.

Declarer's Plan

West's goal is to take ten tricks. There are two sure spades, a diamond, and two sure clubs. Five more tricks are needed.

The heart suit can provide four tricks through promotion, by driving out the defenders' ♥A and ♥K. One more trick might come from the diamond suit with the help of a finesse. Declarer can hope to take a trick with the ♦Q if North holds the ♦K.

In considering the order, de-

DECLARER'S PLAN—THE ABC'S

Declarer: West   Contract: 4♥

ASSESS THE SITUATION

Goal	10
Sure Tricks	5
Extra Tricks Needed	5

BROWSE DECLARER'S CHECKLIST

Promotion	4 in hearts
Length	
The Finesse	1 in diamonds
Trumping in dummy	

CONSIDER THE ORDER

- Draw trumps, even if it requires giving up one or more tricks.
- Lead toward the card you hope will take a trick, the ♦Q.

clarer starts by drawing trumps, even though the defenders have the ♥A and ♥K. Declarer wins the first club and leads a heart. Suppose the defenders win and lead another club. Declarer wins and leads a second heart. The defenders take their second heart trick, but trumps are now drawn. The defenders might now lead a spade. Declarer can take the ♠A and ♠K and trump a spade in the dummy[52].

Declarer must try to get a trick with the ♦Q. The best chance is to take the ♦A and lead a low diamond toward dummy's ♦Q. When North holds the ♦K, the finesse succeeds: if North plays the ♦K on the second round of the suit, dummy's ♦Q is a winner later; If North plays a low diamond, dummy's ♦Q wins the trick.

Comments

Using Jacoby transfers, responder has a straightforward method to invite opener to game in a major when holding a six-card or longer suit. Responder first transfers to the major and then raises to the three level.

---

[52] Eliminating the spade suit between the combined hands, as well as the club suit, actually improves the chances of making the contract. If North's ♦K and South's ♦J were exchanged, the diamond finesse would lose, but South would have nothing left to lead except a spade or a club. This would let declarer trump in the West hand and discard the last diamond from the East hand. This concept is outside the scope of this series.

```
                    ♠ A K J
                    ♥ A K
                    ♦ A K 6 5 3
                    ♣ A 10 5
                 ┌──── NORTH ────┐
   ♠ Q 2         │               │    ♠ 10 9 8 7 5
   ♥ Q 8 4 3     │ WEST     EAST │    ♥ J 7 2
   ♦ Q 10 9 2    │               │    ♦ J 7
   ♣ Q 8 6       │               │    ♣ K 9 2
                 └──── SOUTH ────┘
                    ♠ 6 4 3
                    ♥ 10 9 6 5
                    ♦ 8 4
                    ♣ J 7 4 3
```

Suggested Bidding

WEST	NORTH	EAST	SOUTH
Pass	2♣	Pass	2♦
Pass	3NT	Pass	Pass
Pass			

West passes. North has a balanced hand with 26 high-card points plus 1 length point for the five-card diamond suit. North starts with an artificial strong 2♣ bid.

East passes. South cannot pass the forcing 2♣ bid. South makes an artificial waiting response of 2♦, allowing opener to describe the hand.

North jumps to 3NT to show a balanced hand with about 25–27 points. South doesn't have enough strength to investigate whether the partnership holds an eight-card heart fit. Using the Stayman convention over 3NT might get the partnership too high. South passes and North becomes declarer in 3NT.

Suggested Opening Lead

East leads the ♠10, top of the solid sequence in East's longest suit.

Declarer's Plan

The South hand comes down as the dummy and North's goal is to take nine tricks.

There are two sure spade tricks, two hearts, two diamonds, and one club. Two more tricks are required.

After the spade lead from East, declarer is assured of an extra trick from the ♠J, whether or not West plays the ♠Q. Only one more trick is needed.

DECLARER'S PLAN—THE ABC'S

Declarer: North   Contract: 3NT

ASSESS THE SITUATION

Goal	9
Sure Tricks	7
Extra Tricks Needed	2

BROWSE DECLARER'S CHECKLIST

Promotion	
Length	1 in diamonds
The Finesse	1 in spades

CONSIDER THE ORDER

- Take the losses early when developing the extra diamond trick.

The diamond suit provides the opportunity for one or two extra tricks through length. There are seven diamonds in the combined hands. If the six missing diamonds are divided exactly 3-3—which is unlikely—the diamond suit will provide two extra tricks. If, as is more likely, the six missing diamonds are divided slightly unevenly, 4-2, one extra trick can be developed through length.

After winning the first spade, declarer should go about developing an extra winner in diamonds. It is best to take the losses early, while declarer still has winners in the other suits. Declarer takes the ♦A and ♦K, and plays a third round, giving up a trick to West. East shows out on the third round of diamonds, and declarer now knows the missing diamonds were originally divided 4-2. On regaining the lead, declarer leads another diamond, giving up a second trick to the defenders. When declarer regains the lead, North's remaining diamond is established as a winner and declarer has nine tricks to take.

Comments

Declarer will often have to develop extra tricks through length, perhaps giving up one or more tricks to the defenders. Declarer can expect an even number of missing cards to divide slightly unevenly. An odd number of missing cards will tend to divide as evenly as possible.

DEAL: 21
DEALER: NORTH
VUL: NONE

```
                    ♠ K 6
                    ♥ Q J 10 6 2
                    ♦ 7 5 4
                    ♣ 9 6 3
        NORTH
♠ Q J 10 8 3              ♠ 9 5
♥ 8      WEST   EAST      ♥ 9 7 5 4 3
♦ Q 8 2                   ♦ J 10 9
♣ A 8 4 2    SOUTH        ♣ Q J 10
                    ♠ A 7 4 2
                    ♥ A K
                    ♦ A K 6 3
                    ♣ K 7 5
```

Suggested Bidding

WEST	NORTH	EAST	SOUTH
	Pass	Pass	2NT
Pass	3♦	Pass	3♥
Pass	3NT	Pass	Pass
Pass			

North and East pass. South opens 2NT with a balanced hand and 21 high-card points. West passes.

North has 6 high-card points plus 1 length point for the five-card heart suit. North knows the partnership has enough combined strength for game; the question is WHERE? Since North has a five-card heart suit, the partnership will have an eight-card or longer major suit fit if South has three or more hearts.

North starts with a transfer bid of 3♦, asking opener to bid 3♥. Once South bids 3♥, North offers a choice of games by bidding 3NT. This shows exactly five hearts. With only two hearts, South chooses to play in 3NT by passing. With three or more hearts, South would choose 4♥.

South becomes declarer in 3NT.

Suggested Opening Lead

West leads the ♠Q, top of the solid sequence, against South's 3NT contract.

Declarer's Plan

South's goal is to take nine tricks. South counts the sure tricks. There are two sure spade tricks, five sure heart tricks, and two diamond tricks. South has all the tricks that are needed.

With enough tricks to make the contract, declarer's plan is to take the tricks and run. That sounds easy enough, but sometimes declarer has to be careful about the order in which the tricks are taken.

```
┌─ DECLARER'S PLAN—THE ABC'S ─┐

Declarer: South   Contract: 3NT

ASSESS THE SITUATION
Goal                 9
Sure Tricks          9
Extra Tricks Needed  0

BROWSE DECLARER'S CHECKLIST
Promotion
Length
The Finesse

CONSIDER THE ORDER
• Use high crads wisely to get from
  one side of the table to the other.
```

Suppose declarer wins the first trick with dummy's ♠K. Declarer can then take the ♥A-K, ♦A-K, and ♠A, but runs into a problem in taking the last three heart winners. They are in the dummy but there is no way to get to them. They are stranded.

To overcome this challenge, declarer must win the first trick with the ♠A, keeping the ♠K in the dummy. Declarer can then take the ♥A-K and use the ♠K as an entry to get over to the dummy and take the ♥Q-J-10. The ♦A-K are the other two winners declarer needs to take the first nine tricks and move on to the next deal.

Comments

When taking winners in an unevenly divided suit, it is sometimes important to keep a high-card, an entry, on the same side of the table as the long suit.

DEAL: 22

DEALER: EAST

VUL: N-S

NORTH
- ♠ 10 7 5 3
- ♥ 10 9 8 5 3
- ♦ 6 2
- ♣ 8 2

WEST
- ♠ J 2
- ♥ Q 7 6
- ♦ 9 3
- ♣ A Q 10 9 7 5

EAST
- ♠ A K Q
- ♥ J
- ♦ A K J 7 4
- ♣ K J 6 3

SOUTH
- ♠ 9 8 6 4
- ♥ A K 4 2
- ♦ Q 10 8 5
- ♣ 4

Suggested Bidding

WEST	NORTH	EAST	SOUTH
		2♣	Pass
3♣	Pass	4NT	Pass
5♦	Pass	6♣	Pass
Pass	Pass		

East has 22 high-card points plus 1 length point for the five-card diamond suit. East opens an artificial strong 2♣ bid. South passes.

West has a good six-card suit with two of the top three high cards in the suit. West also has 9 high-card points. That's enough to make a positive response of 3♣, instead of the 2♦ waiting bid.

East now knows the partnership has a suitable trump fit in clubs, so there is no need to look for a fit elsewhere. East can also visualize a slam contract if the partnership is not missing two aces. So, East jumps to 4NT, the Blackwood convention, asking for the number of aces held by West[53].

West's 5♦ reply to the Blackwood convention shows one ace and tells East that the partnership is missing only one ace. That's okay for a small slam, so East puts the partnership in 6♣.

---

[53] By inference, East's jump to 4NT implies that the partnership has a fit in clubs and that clubs is the agreed trump suit.

Suggested Opening Lead

South leads the ♥A, top of the touching cards, against East's 6♣ contract.

Declarer's Plan

East's goal is to take twelve tricks. There are three sure tricks in spades, two in diamonds, and six in clubs. One more trick is required.

On this deal, declarer can get the extra trick in a number of ways. If South plays the ♥K after winning the ♥A, declarer will trump in the East hand and dummy's ♥Q will be a winner. Even if South doesn't lead a second heart, declarer can trump a

+--- DECLARER'S PLAN—THE ABC'S ---+

Declarer: East   Contract: 6♣

ASSESS THE SITUATION
Goal   12
Sure Tricks   11
Extra Tricks Needed   1

BROWSE DECLARER'S CHECKLIST
Promotion
Length
The Finesse
Trumping in dummy[54] 1 in hearts

CONSIDER THE ORDER
• Keep enough trumps in the East

heart in the East hand[54] at a later point. That will give declarer an extra trump trick and enough tricks to make the contract.

Declarer loses only one heart trick.

Comments

Once a trump fit is found, East can use the Blackwood convention to make sure that the defenders cannot take the first two tricks against a small slam contract.

---

[54] Although the East hand is not actually the dummy on this deal, East has become declarer because of the artificial 2♣ opening. Trumping in the hand with fewer trumps has the same effect as trumping in the dummy. It gains a trick.

DEAL: 23
DEALER: SOUTH
VUL: E-W

NORTH
- ♠ 10 4 3
- ♥ 9 7 3
- ♦ K J 10 9 3
- ♣ J 4

WEST
- ♠ A J 9 7
- ♥ Q J 10 6
- ♦ A 6
- ♣ K 6 3

EAST
- ♠ K Q 8 5
- ♥ K 5 2
- ♦ 8 4
- ♣ A 8 5 2

SOUTH
- ♠ 6 2
- ♥ A 8 4
- ♦ Q 7 5 2
- ♣ Q 10 9 7

Suggested Bidding

WEST	NORTH	EAST	SOUTH
			Pass
1NT	Pass	2♣	Pass
2♥	Pass	3NT	Pass
4♠	Pass	Pass	Pass

After South passes, West opens 1NT with a balanced hand and 15 high-card points. North passes.

East has 12 high-card points, enough to take the partnership to game. With a four-card spade suit, East uses the Stayman convention to ask if opener has a four-card major.

With both major suits, West replies 2♥ to the Stayman convention, bidding four-card suits 'up the line.' That isn't the major suit that East was interested in, so East now jumps to 3NT.

West can infer that East must have been interested in spades. East used the Stayman convention, but was not interested in hearts. So West can bid 4♠, putting the partnership in its eight-card major suit fit. East passes, and the partnership has found the best contract.

Suggested Opening Lead

Against West's 4♠ contract, North might choose to lead the ♦J, top of the interior sequence in diamonds.

Declarer's Plan

After North leads, East puts down the dummy and West makes a plan. The goal is to take ten tricks. There are four sure spade tricks, one diamond, and two clubs. Three more tricks are needed.

Declarer browses the checklist. Declarer can plan to develop three winners in the heart suit through promotion.

After winning a trick with the ♦A, declarer's first task is

```
┌─ DECLARER'S PLAN—THE ABC'S ─┐
 Declarer: West     Contract: 4♠
 ASSESS THE SITUATION
 Goal                  10
 Sure Tricks            7
 Extra Tricks Needed    3

 BROWSE DECLARER'S CHECKLIST
 Promotion          3 in hearts
 Length
 The Finesse
 Trumping in dummy

 CONSIDER THE ORDER
  • Draw trumps.
  • Take the loss in hearts early
```

to draw trumps. This takes three rounds of spades. Once this is done, declarer can go about developing the extra winners in hearts by driving out the defenders' ♥A.

After South wins the ♥A, the defenders can take one diamond trick, but that's all before having to give the lead back to declarer. Declarer takes the remaining winners, and the defenders get a club trick at the end. Ten tricks for declarer.

Comments

The key on this deal is for East-West to find the eight-card spade fit by using the Stayman convention. If East-West reach 3NT instead of 4♠, North-South can defeat the contract. North can lead the ♦J and the defenders will establish four diamond tricks. They will also get a trick with the ♥A.

	♠ AKJ95
DEAL: 24	**♥ 5**
DEALER: WEST	**♦ KQJ63**
VUL: BOTH	**♣ KQ**

```
              NORTH
♠  8 6 3                      ♠  2
♥  10 8 4 3   WEST    EAST    ♥  K Q J 6
♦  9                          ♦  10 8 7 4 2
♣  A J 7 5 2                  ♣  10 8 4
              SOUTH
```

♠ Q 10 7 4
♥ A 9 7 2
♦ A 5
♣ 9 6 3

Suggested Bidding

WEST	NORTH	EAST	SOUTH
Pass	1♠	Pass	3♠
Pass	4NT	Pass	5♥
Pass	6♠	Pass	Pass
Pass			

West passes. North has 19 high-card points plus two length points for the two five-card suits. That's not quite enough for a strong 2♣ opening, so North bids the higher-ranking of the two five-card suits, 1♠. East passes.

South has four-card support for spades and 10 high-card points plus 1 dummy point for the doubleton diamond. That's enough for a jump raise to 3♠. This is an invitational, limit, raise, showing about 11–12 points.

North now knows WHERE the partnership belongs, spades. Since South has shown about 11–12 points and North holds 21, the partnership is in the slam range with a combined total of 32–33 points. North's hand suggests that the partnership should have a good chance at making 6♠ if it is not missing two aces. So, North uses the Blackwood convention.

South's 5♥ response shows two aces. North now knows the partnership is missing one ace, but not two. That's okay for a small slam. North takes the partnership to 6♠.

Suggested Opening Lead

Against the slam contract. East leads the ♥K, top of the solid sequence.

Declarer's Plan

North's goal is to take at least twelve tricks. North can count on five sure tricks in spades and one in hearts. Assuming the missing diamonds are divided 3-3 or 4-2, there are also five sure tricks in diamonds[55]. That's a total of eleven tricks. One more is needed.

South browses Declarer's Checklist for ways to develop the extra trick. A trick can be promoted in clubs by driving out the ♣A.

```
┌ DECLARER'S PLAN—THE ABC'S ┐
  Declarer: North    Contract: 6♠

  ASSESS THE SITUATION
  Goal                12
  Sure Tricks         11
  Extra Tricks Needed  1

  BROWSE DECLARER'S CHECKLIST
  Promotion          1 in clubs
  Length
  The Finesse
  Trumping in dummy

  CONSIDER THE ORDER
  • Draw trumps.
  • Take the loss early in clubs.
```

Declarer wins the first trick with dummy's ♥A. The first task is to draw the defenders' trumps. Once that is done, declarer can lead the ♣K or ♣Q to promote a trick in clubs. By taking the loss early, declarer has no problem regaining the lead and taking the rest of the tricks, making the small slam contract.

Comments

The partnership reaches the small slam contract with the help of the Blackwood convention. The partnership does not want to be in a slam contract missing two aces. It's okay to be missing one ace in a small slam contract, provided the partnership has enough combined strength to have a good chance of taking twelve tricks.

[55] Even if the missing diamonds were divided 5-1 or 6-0, North could trump a diamond in the dummy.

♠ K J 4
♥ 9 3
♦ K 9 8 6 3
♣ 10 7 5

DEAL: 25
DEALER: NORTH
VUL: NONE

♠ A 8 7　　　　　　　　　　　♠ Q 9 5 3
♥ K J 8 5　　　　　　　　　　♥ Q 10 7 4
♦ A J　　　　　　　　　　　　♦ 10 4
♣ A K Q J　　　　　　　　　　♣ 9 6 2

♠ 10 6 2
♥ A 6 2
♦ Q 7 5 2
♣ 8 4 3

Suggested Bidding

WEST	NORTH	EAST	SOUTH
	PASS	PASS	PASS
2♣	PASS	2♦	PASS
2NT	PASS	3♣	PASS
3♥	PASS	4♥	PASS
PASS	PASS		

North, East, and South all pass. West has a balanced hand with 23 high-card points. That's too strong to open 2NT, so West starts with the artificial strong 2♣ bid. North passes.

East makes a waiting response of 2♦. After South passes, West describes the hand with a rebid of 2NT. This shows a balanced hand of 22–24 points.

Although West's bid of 2NT is not forcing, East has 4 high-card points, enough to take the partnership to a game contract. With four cards in each major, there is the possibility that the partnership has an eight-card major suit fit. So East makes use of the Stayman convention by bidding 3♣.

West replies to the Stayman convention by bidding 3♥ to show the four-card heart suit. East now knows both How High and Where the partnership belongs and raises to 4♥.

Suggested Opening Lead

North has no clearcut lead against the 4♥ contract. North might choose the ♦6, fourth highest from the long suit.

Declarer's Plan

West's goal is to take ten tricks with hearts as the trump suit. There is a spade trick, a diamond, and four club tricks. Four more tricks need to be developed.

Three tricks can be developed through promotion in the heart suit. In addition, there is the possibility of getting an extra trick from the ♠Q with the help of a finesse.

In considering the order, declarer's priority is to draw

<table>
<tr><td colspan="2">── DECLARER'S PLAN—THE ABC'S ──</td></tr>
<tr><td>Declarer: West</td><td>Contract: 4♥</td></tr>
<tr><td colspan="2">Assess the Situation</td></tr>
<tr><td>Goal</td><td>10</td></tr>
<tr><td>Sure Tricks</td><td>6</td></tr>
<tr><td>Extra Tricks Needed</td><td>4</td></tr>
<tr><td colspan="2">Browse Declarer's Checklist</td></tr>
<tr><td>Promotion</td><td>3 in hearts</td></tr>
<tr><td>Length</td><td></td></tr>
<tr><td>The Finesse</td><td>1 in spades</td></tr>
<tr><td>Trumping in dummy</td><td></td></tr>
<tr><td colspan="2">Consider the Order</td></tr>
<tr><td colspan="2">• Draw trumps.</td></tr>
<tr><td colspan="2">• Lead toward the ♠Q, the card you hope will take a trick.</td></tr>
</table>

trumps. Since the ♥A is missing, Declarer starts by using a high heart to drive out the defenders' ♥A. After South wins the ♥A, the defenders can take one diamond trick, but that's all before declarer can regain the lead.

Declarer finishes drawing trumps, which takes two more rounds of hearts. Then declarer turns attention to the spade suit. Declarer has to hope that North holds the ♠K. Declarer takes the ♠A and leads toward the ♠Q, the card declarer hopes will take a trick. On this deal, the finesse works because North holds the ♠K. If North takes the ♠K, East's ♠Q will be a trick after regaining the lead; if North doesn't play the ♠K, declarer immediately wins a trick with the ♠Q.

Comments

The Stayman convention can be used after an opening bid of 2♣, a 2♦ waiting response, and a 2NT rebid. On this deal, it is important for East-West to play in their eight-card heart fit. A contract of 3NT can be defeated if the defenders lead diamonds to establish four winners to go with their ♥A.

DEAL: 26	♠ A 8 7 5 2	
DEALER: EAST	♥ Q 10 9 6 3	
VUL: N-S	♦ 5	
	♣ Q 9	

```
              NORTH
♠ 6 3                      ♠ K Q 10 9
♥ A 7      WEST   EAST     ♥ 8 4
♦ K J 10 9 6               ♦ A 8 4 2
♣ 8 5 4 2                  ♣ 10 7 3
              SOUTH
```

♠ J 4
♥ K J 5 2
♦ Q 7 3
♣ A K J 6

Suggested Bidding

WEST	NORTH	EAST	SOUTH
		Pass	1NT
Pass	2♥	Pass	2♠
Pass	3♥	Pass	4♥
Pass	Pass	Pass	

South, with a balanced hand and 15 high-card points, opens 1NT.

North has 8 high-card points plus 1 point for each five-card suit. The total of 10 points is enough to take the partnership to the game level. With five cards in both major suits, North wants to find an eight-card or longer major suit fit.

North starts with 2♥, transferring opener to spades After South bids 2♠, North shows the second suit by bidding 3♥. The 3♥ bid is forcing, asking opener to choose between spades and hearts[56].

With four-card support for hearts, South puts the partnership in 4♥.

Suggested Opening Lead

East leads the ♠K, top of the broken sequence in spades[57].

---

[56] Transferring to spades and then bidding hearts shows at least five cards in both major suits. With a four-card major, responder would start with the Stayman convention, even with five or more cards in the other major suit.

[57] Since North has shown at least five spades in the auction, East might choose to lead another suit.

Declarer's Plan

North's goal is to take at least ten tricks. There is one sure trick in spades and four in clubs. Five more tricks are required.

North browses Declarer's Checklist. Four tricks can be promoted in the heart suit. Since there are more spades in the North hand than in the dummy, declarer can also plan to trump at least one spade in dummy.

After winning the first trick with the ♠A, declarer can start by drawing trumps[58]. To draw trumps, declarer must drive out the ♥A to promote the other hearts as winners, and then draw the remaining trumps in the defenders' hands after regaining the lead.

After drawing trumps, declarer can give up a spade trick to the opponents and then trump a spade in dummy after regaining the lead. Declarer's remaining spades can be discarded on dummy's club winners. Declarer loses only one spade trick, one heart, and one diamond.

DECLARER'S PLAN—THE ABC'S		
Declarer: North		Contract: 4♥
ASSESS THE SITUATION		
Goal		10
Sure Tricks		5
Extra Tricks Needed		5
BROWSE DECLARER'S CHECKLIST		
Promotion		4 in hearts
Length		
The Finesse		
Trumping in dummy		1 in spades
CONSIDER THE ORDER		
• Draw trumps.		
• Keep a heart in dummy to trump a spade.		

Comments

Stayman is used when responder has at least one four-card major suit. Jacoby transfer bids are used when responder has at least a five-card or longer major suit. Jacoby transfers can be used to show a two-suited hand with 10 or more points by first transferring to the higher-ranking suit and then bidding the lower ranking suit.

---

[58] If East leads a spade, declarer can make an overtrick on the actual layout by winning the ♠A, playing the ♣Q, and then taking two more club winners, discarding the ♦5 from the North hand. Declarer can later trump two spades in the dummy. Taking three club winners before drawing trumps runs the risk of being defeated, if a defender has a singleton club.

DEAL: 27
DEALER: SOUTH
VUL: E-W

♠ 3
♥ K 7
♦ A J 2
♣ K Q 10 9 7 6 3

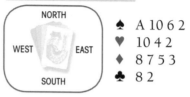

♠ 9 7 5 4
♥ A 9 8 5 3
♦ 10 6
♣ A 4

♠ A 10 6 2
♥ 10 4 2
♦ 8 7 5 3
♣ 8 2

♠ K Q J 8
♥ Q J 6
♦ K Q 9 4
♣ J 5

Suggested Bidding

WEST	NORTH	EAST	SOUTH
			1NT
Pass	4♣	Pass	4♦
Pass	4NT	Pass	Pass
Pass			

South is the dealer and has a balanced hand with 15 high-card points. South opens 1NT. West passes.

North has 13 high-card points plus 3 length points for the seven-card club suit. North can visualize that the partnership might be able to make a slam if South has at least two aces. To find out how many aces South holds, North uses the Gerber convention, 4♣.

South's reply to the Gerber convention is 4♦, showing no aces[59]. North now knows that the partnership is missing three aces. Even a game contract of 5♣ would be in danger, since the defenders could take the first three tricks[60]. So, North signs off in a contract of 4NT. Even though North's hand is unbalanced, the partnership should hold enough strength to make ten tricks in notrump, since it can't be missing much more than the three aces.

South passes North's signoff bid, ending the auction.

---

[59] The 4♦ reply shows zero or four aces. Holding an ace, North can infer that South holds zero.
[60] North can't sign off in 5♣, since that would be a continuation of the Gerber convention, asking how many kings opener holds.

Suggested Opening Lead

West would lead the ♥5, fourth highest from the longest suit, against the 4NT contract.

Declarer's Plan

South's goal is to take ten tricks. There are four sure tricks in diamonds, but that's all. Six more tricks are needed.

Declarer browses the checklist. There are three suits that offer the possibility of developing extra winners through promotion. Two tricks can be promoted in the spade suit, two in the heart suit, and six in the club suit.

In considering the order,

```
┌─ DECLARER'S PLAN—THE ABC'S ─┐

  Declarer: South   Contract: 4NT

  ASSESS THE SITUATION
  Goal                    10
  Sure Tricks              4
  Extra Tricks Needed   6

  BROWSE DECLARER'S CHECKLIST
  Promotion            6 in clubs
                       2 in spades
                       2 in hearts
  Length
  The Finesse

  CONSIDER THE ORDER
  • Take the losses early when prompt-
    ing winners.
```

South needs to be aware that the defenders are also trying to develop tricks—through length in the heart suit on this deal. South won't have time to promote winners in all three suits. So South should go after the suit that provides all the necessary winners, clubs.

After winning the first heart trick, declarer immediately leads clubs to drive out the defenders' ♣A. The defenders can take three tricks in total with their three aces, but that's all. On regaining the lead, declarer can take enough tricks in clubs and diamonds to make the contract.

Comments

The Gerber convention, 4♣, is used to ask about aces immediately over an opening bid of 1NT. When using this convention, responder needs to know how to stop safely below the slam level if the partnership does not have enough aces. 4NT is often used as a signoff after Gerber when responder discovers there are not enough aces to go for a slam contract.

DEAL: 28	♠ 6 4 2		
DEALER: WEST	♥ 8 4 3		
VUL: BOTH	♦ A 2		
	♣ K 10 7 6 3		

```
                      ♠ 6 4 2
                      ♥ 8 4 3
                      ♦ A 2
                      ♣ K 10 7 6 3
                         NORTH
  ♠ K J 9                            ♠ A Q 7 5
  ♥ A J 7         WEST       EAST    ♥ K Q 9 5 2
  ♦ K Q 7 3                          ♦ 6 5 4
  ♣ J 5 2            SOUTH           ♣ 8
                      ♠ 10 8 3
                      ♥ 10 6
                      ♦ J 10 9 8
                      ♣ A Q 9 4
```

Suggested Bidding

WEST	NORTH	EAST	SOUTH
1NT	PASS	2♣	PASS
2♦	PASS	3♥	PASS
4♥	PASS	PASS	PASS

West is the dealer and opens 1NT with a balanced hand and 15 high-card points. North passes.

East has 11 high-card points plus 1 length point for the five-card heart suit. East knows the partnership has enough combined strength for game. The only question is WHERE? Holding a four-card major in spades, East uses the Stayman convention, even when holding a five-card heart suit. If West shows four cards in either major, East will be able to raise to the game level.

With no four-card major, West replies 2♦ to the Stayman inquiry. East now knows the partnership doesn't have an eight-card fit in spades, but there is still the possibility of an eight-card fit in hearts. To find out if opener has three-card support for hearts, East now jumps to 3♥, asking opener to choose between game in 3NT or 4♥.

With three-card support for hearts, West puts the partnership in 4♥. East becomes the declarer.

Suggested Opening Lead

South leads the ♦J, top of the solid sequence, against East's 4♥ contract.

Declarer's Plan

East's goal is to take ten tricks with hearts as the trump suit. East counts the sure tricks. There are four in spades and five in hearts. One more trick is needed.

East browses Declarer's Checklist. East can plan to promote the extra trick in diamonds[61]. If South leads the ♦J, declarer will get the work done early.

Declarer plays the ♦Q or ♦K

┌─ DECLARER'S PLAN—THE ABC'S ─┐

Declarer: East   Contract: 4♥

ASSESS THE SITUATION

Goal	10
Sure Tricks	9
Extra Tricks Needed	1

BROWSE DECLARER'S CHECKLIST

Promotion	1 in diamonds
Length	
The Finesse	
Trumping in dummy	

CONSIDER THE ORDER
- Draw trumps.
- Take the loss early in diamonds.

on South's lead of the ♦J. After North wins the ♦A, West's remaining high diamond is promoted into a winner. After gaining the lead, declarer can draw the defenders' trumps and take the spade winners along with the promoted diamond trick.

The defenders will later get a second diamond trick as well as a club trick, but that's all. Declarer has the ten tricks needed to make 4♥.

Comments

Responder is often faced with the decision about whether to use Stayman or Jacoby transfers to find a major suit fit. Holding at least one four-card major, responder should start with the Stayman convention.

If East-West were to play in 3NT on this deal, the defenders can take the first five club tricks to defeat the contract.

---

[61] In theory, declarer might get two diamond tricks from this holding with the help of a repeated finesse—leading twice toward dummy's ♦K and ♦Q—if South holds the ♦A. In practice, South is unlikely to hold the ♦A after leading the ♦J against a suit contract.

DEAL: 29	♠ K J 5		
DEALER: NORTH	♥ K 9 3		
VUL: NONE	♦ K Q J		
	♣ A 8 6 3		

♠ A 10 9 8
♥ A 10 7
♦ 8 6
♣ Q 7 5 4

NORTH
WEST   EAST
SOUTH

♠ 6 3
♥ J 6 2
♦ A 4 3
♣ K J 10 9 2

♠ Q 7 4 2
♥ Q 8 5 4
♦ 10 9 7 5 2
♣ —

Suggested Bidding

WEST	NORTH	EAST	SOUTH
	1NT	PASS	2♣
PASS	2♦	PASS	PASS
PASS			

North is the dealer and has a balanced hand with 17 high-card points. North opens 1NT. East passes.

South has only 4 high-card points plus 1 length point for the five-card diamond suit. South knows How High, partscore. The only decision is Where? Responder usually needs at least 8 points to use the Stayman convention, at least enough to invite the partnership to game. An exception can be made, however, when responder is short in clubs. On this type of hand, it is safe for South to respond 2♣. If North bids 2♥ or 2♠, South can pass and the partnership will have landed in partscore in an eight-card fit. If North bids 2♦, South can also pass, leaving the partnership in a partscore in diamonds.

On the actual deal, North replies 2♦ to the Stayman inquiry and South passes. South's pass of 2♦ might be a surprise to North, but the partnership has actually found an eight-card fit[62].

---

[62] If North held only two diamonds, the partnership would be in a seven-card fit. That still might be a better contract than 1NT.

Suggested Opening Lead

Against 2♦, East might lead the ♣J, top of the interior sequence in clubs.

Declarer's Plan

North's goal is to take at least eight tricks with diamonds as the trump suit.

North starts with only one sure trick, the ♣A. Seven more tricks need to be developed.

Three suits offer the possibility of promotion. Two tricks can be promoted in spades, one in hearts, and four in diamonds.

There is also the possibility of trumping clubs in dummy. However, since dummy has more diamonds than declarer,

```
┌─ DECLARER'S PLAN—THE ABC'S ─┐

  Declarer: North    Contract: 2♦

  ASSESS THE SITUATION
  Goal                    8
  Sure Tricks             1
  Extra Tricks Needed     7

  BROWSE DECLARER'S CHECKLIST
  Promotion          2 in spades
                     1 in hearts
                     4 in diamonds
  Length
  The Finesse
  Trumping in dummy  ?

  CONSIDER THE ORDER
  • Take the losses early when promot-
    ing winners.
```

this will not usually gain tricks. Declarer has already counted four tricks from diamonds through promotion, so trumping a club in dummy just reduces the number of tricks available from promotion[63].

Declarer can win the ♣A and start by driving out the ♦A. This promotes winners and draws trumps at the same time. Declarer can then drive out both the ♠A and ♥A to promote the additional tricks needed.

Comments

The Stayman convention can be used by responder with fewer than 8 points when responder is short in clubs. This is safe because responder can pass any reply and stop safely in a reasonable partscore.

On this deal, South does well to get the partnership to 2♦ instead of passing 1NT. East-West can defeat 1NT by promoting four winners in clubs and taking their three aces.

---

[63] Technically, declarer can gain a trick by trumping enough clubs in dummy so that declarer has more diamonds than dummy, but this is not necessary on this deal.

		♠	2
		♥	Q J 10 7 5 4
		♦	2
		♣	10 6 4 3 2

DEAL: 30
DEALER: EAST
VUL: N-S

♠ A Q J 9 4
♥ A K 3
♦ 8 3
♣ K Q 8

NORTH

WEST   EAST

SOUTH

♠ K 10 7 5
♥ 9 2
♦ A K J 6 4
♣ A J

♠ 8 6 3
♥ 8 6
♦ Q 10 9 7 5
♣ 9 7 5

Suggested Bidding

WEST	NORTH	EAST	SOUTH
		1♦	PASS
1♠	PASS	3♠	PASS
4NT	PASS	5♥	PASS
5NT	PASS	6♥	PASS
7♠	PASS	PASS	PASS

East has 16 high-card points plus 1 length point for the five-card suit. Since there are two doubletons, the hand is unbalanced. So, East opens the longest suit, 1♦.

South passes. West has 19 high-card points plus 1 length point for the five-card suit. Since East has shown at least 13 points by opening the bidding, West knows the partnership has at least 33 combined points and is headed for the slam level. However, West does not yet know WHERE the partnership belongs. So, West starts by bidding 1♠[64], the long suit. North passes.

East has four-card support for spades and a medium-strength hand. East shows both the support and extra strength by jumping to 3♠. A raise to only 2♠ would show a minimum opening bid.

---

[64] West could make a strong jump shift to 2♠, showing about 19 or more points. However, that takes up a lot of bidding room which might better be used to find out Where the partnership belongs. The 1♠ response is forcing. West can show the extra strength later.

West now knows WHERE the partnership belongs, spades. Since East has shown about 17–18 points, the only remaining question is whether the partnership can make a grand slam. West uses the Blackwood convention, 4NT, to check that the partnership holds all the aces.

East's 5♥ reply shows two aces. West has two, so the partnership isn't missing an ace. With interest in a grand slam, West continues with Blackwood by bidding 5NT to ask about kings.

East's 6♥ reply shows two kings. West now knows the partnership holds all the aces and kings and about 37 combined points. That's enough to go for a grand slam. West puts the partnership in 7♠.

Suggested Opening Lead

North leads the ♥Q, top of the solid sequence.

Declarer's Plan

West's goal is to take all thirteen tricks. There are five sure spade tricks, two hearts, two diamonds, and three clubs. One more trick is required.

Diamonds could provide an extra trick through a finesse or length. However, a better plan is to trump a heart in dummy.

Declarer draws trumps, leaving a spade in dummy. Now declarer takes the other heart winner, leads the ♥3 and trumps it in dummy. Declarer has all the remaining tricks.

— DECLARER'S PLAN—THE ABC'S —

Declarer: West   Contract: 7♠

ASSESS THE SITUATION
Goal   13
Sure Tricks   12
Extra Tricks Needed   1

BROWSE DECLARER'S CHECKLIST
Promotion
Length
The Finesse
Trumping in dummy 1 in hearts

CONSIDER THE ORDER
- Draw trumps.
- Leave a spade in the dummy to trump a heart.

Comments

Once the partnership is headed for a slam contract, Blackwood can be used to check that the partnership is not missing any important cards. If the partnership has all the aces and is interested in reaching a grand slam, a bid of 5NT can be used to check whether the partnership is missing any kings.

DEAL: 31
DEALER: SOUTH
VUL: E-W

♠ J 6 3
♥ 7 3
♦ 8 7 5 3
♣ 10 7 4 2

♠ 9 7 4
♥ Q 9 2
♦ A K 10 9
♣ 8 5 3

NORTH
WEST   EAST
SOUTH

♠ A 8 5 2
♥ 10 4
♦ Q 6 4 2
♣ Q J 9

♠ K Q 10
♥ A K J 8 6 5
♦ J
♣ A K 6

Suggested Bidding

WEST	NORTH	EAST	SOUTH
			2♣
Pass	2♦	Pass	2♥
Pass	3♣	Pass	3♥
Pass	Pass	Pass	

South has 21 high-card points plus 2 length points for the six-card heart suit. That's enough strength to open with an artificial strong 2♣ bid. West passes.

North has a very weak hand with only 1 point, but North can't pass the forcing 2♣ bid. North makes an artificial waiting response of 2♦. East passes.

South now starts describing the hand by bidding 2♥. This shows an unbalanced hand with 22 or more points and a five-card or longer heart suit.

South's 2♥ bid is forcing, since South's strength is unlimited. North must bid again. To show a very weak hand, North bids an artificial 3♣, the cheaper minor suit available at the three level.

With no second suit to bid and nothing much extra for the strong 2♣ bid, South rebids 3♥. South's rebid in the same suit after North has shown a very weak hand is not forcing. North can finally pass, and the partnership stops in partscore.

Suggested Opening Lead

Against South's 3♥ contract, West leads the ♦A, top of the touching high cards in the suit.

Declarer's Plan

South's goal as declarer is to take nine tricks. There are two sure hearts and two sure clubs. Five more tricks are needed.

Two tricks can be developed through promotion in spades. The rest will have to come from hearts. If the five missing hearts are divided 3-2, the heart suit will provide three extra tricks through length. There is also the possibility that the ♥Q will fall under the ♥A or ♥K[65].

┌─ DECLARER'S PLAN—THE ABC'S ─┐

Declarer: South   Contract: 3♥

ASSESS THE SITUATION

Goal	9
Sure Tricks	4
Extra Tricks Needed	5

BROWSE DECLARER'S CHECKLIST

Promotion	2 in spades
Length	3 in hearts
The Finesse	
Trumping in dummy	

CONSIDER THE ORDER
- Draw trumps first.
- Take the loss early in spades.

If West leads the ♦A and ♦K, declarer can trump the second round. Then declarer can draw two rounds of trumps with the ♥A and ♥K. The ♥Q doesn't fall. However, it is the only high heart outstanding. Declarer can simply start promoting the extra winners in spades, letting the defenders take the ♥Q whenever they want.

Comments

The artificial 2♦ response to the 2♣ opening bid is a waiting bid. It doesn't say much about responder's hand, except that it is unsuitable for a positive response. When opener shows an unbalanced hand, responder must bid again. Responder shows a weak hand by using the artificial bid of the cheaper minor suit at the three level. If opener now rebids the same suit, responder can pass.

4♥ is not a hopeless contract for North-South. It would make if either defender held the doubleton ♥Q. On the actual layout, however, North-South do well to stop in 3♥.

---

[65] Ideally, declarer would like to take a finesse in the heart suit, hoping East holds the ♥Q. On this deal, however, declarer has no sure entry to the dummy.

DEAL: 32

DEALER: WEST
VUL: BOTH

♠ A 7 4
♥ Q 10 8 5 2
♦ K 4
♣ 9 6 4

NORTH

♠ K Q 8 5
♥ A K 7 4
♦ 9 6
♣ K Q 7

WEST   EAST

♠ 6 3 2
♥ 6
♦ Q J 10 7 5 3 2
♣ 5 3

SOUTH

♠ J 10 9
♥ J 9 3
♦ A 8
♣ A J 10 8 2

Suggested Bidding

WEST	NORTH	EAST	SOUTH
1NT	PASS	2♠	PASS
3♣	PASS	3♦	PASS
PASS	PASS		

West is the dealer and has 17 high-card points and a balanced hand. West opens 1NT. North passes.

East has only 3 high-card points plus 3 length points for the seven-card diamond suit. East knows HOW HIGH, partscore. East also knows, WHERE. East wants the long diamond suit to be the trump suit. A response of 2♦ would be a transfer to hearts. Instead, East makes the artificial response of 2♠, asking opener to bid 3♣.

West bids 3♣, as requested. Now East bids 3♦. This is a signoff bid in diamonds. West passes, again as requested. The partnerships arrives in a partscore of 3♦ with East as the declarer.

Suggested Opening Lead

South leads the ♠J, top of the solid sequence, against East's 3♦ contract.

Declarer's Plan

East's goal is to take nine tricks. East counts the sure tricks. There are only two, the ♥A-K. Seven more tricks are needed.

All the necessary extra tricks can be developed through promotion. The spade suit can provide a trick. The diamonds can provide five tricks, once the ♦A and ♦K are driven out. The clubs can provide a trick.

The club suit might provide more than one trick with the help of a repeated finesse, by leading twice toward dummy's

DECLARER'S PLAN—THE ABC'S		
Declarer: West	Contract: 3♦	
ASSESS THE SITUATION		
Goal		9
Sure Tricks		2
Extra Tricks Needed		7
BROWSE DECLARER'S CHECKLIST		
Promotion		1 in spades
		5 in diamonds
		1 in clubs
Length		
The Finesse		
Trumping in dummy		
CONSIDER THE ORDER		
• Delay drawing trumps if the defenders have too many winners to take.		

♣K-Q, hoping South holds the ♣A. However, that isn't necessary.

There is a danger, however, that the defenders could take five tricks before declarer can take nine. Suppose South leads the ♠J, declarer plays dummy's ♠Q, or ♠K, and North wins the ♠A. North may lead another spade. Declarer wins, but now the defenders have established a second spade winner. If South leads diamonds right away, the defenders can win and take their spade winner.

To prevent this, declarer can delay drawing trumps. Instead, declarer takes dummy's ♥A and ♥K. On the second heart winner, East discards the remaining low spade. Now it is safe to lead diamonds. The defenders can't get a second spade winner because declarer can ruff. They only get one spade trick, two diamonds, and the ♣A.

Comments

Although declarer can usually develop enough tricks to make the contract, there is often a danger that the defenders may first establish and take enough tricks to defeat the contract. It is a race. Declarer may sometimes have to delay drawing trumps when other considerations take a higher priority. This type of situation will be discussed in more detail in the next book in this series, Declarer Play.

Appendices

Appendix 1 – The ABC's of Declarer Play

When the auction is over, the *opening lead* is made, and dummy is placed face up on the table, declarer should make a plan for taking enough tricks to make the contract. There are three suggested stages, the ABC's:

Declarer's Plan—The ABC's

Assess the Situation
Browse Declarer's Checklist to Develop Extra Tricks
Consider the Order

Assess the Situation

This stage can be divided into three steps:

1) Goal. Start by considering the number of tricks required to make the contract. In 4♥, for example, declarer needs to take ten tricks.

2) Sure Tricks[66]. Count the sure tricks, or *winners*—those that can be taken without giving up the lead. An ace is a sure trick; an ace and king in the same suit are two sure tricks.

3) Extra Tricks Needed. Compare the number of tricks needed to the sure tricks. If there are eight sure tricks in a contract of 4♥, for example, two more are needed.

Browse Declarer's Checklist to Develop Extra Tricks

When there aren't enough sure tricks to make the contract, declarer looks at the various techniques for developing, or establishing, extra tricks:

DECLARER"S CHECKLIST	
Promotion	
Length	
The Finesse	
Trumping in Dummy	

The first three methods are available in both notrump and trump contracts. The fourth is only available in trump contracts.

PROMOTION

Declarer can sometimes turn cards into winners by driving out the higher-ranking cards. For example:

DUMMY
♥ 4 2

DECLARER
♥ K Q

Declarer can lead the ♥K, or ♥Q, to drive out the defenders' ♥A and promote the remaining high card into a winner.

---

[66] In a trump contract, declarer can also count *losers*—the tricks that could be lost to the defenders. This is discussed in more detail in the book on DECLARER PLAY.

LENGTH

If declarer continues to lead a suit until the defenders have no cards left, declarer's remaining cards in the suit become winners.

DUMMY	Declarer can take two sure tricks with the ♦A
♦ 9 6 3	and ♦K and then lead a third round of diamonds, giving up a trick to the defenders. If the five
DECLARER	missing diamonds are divided 3-2, declarer's two
♦ A K 7 5 2	remaining diamonds are winners.

In predicting how many tricks can be developed from a suit through length, declarer can use the guideline:

An odd number of missing cards tends to divide as evenly as possible; an even number of missing cards tends to divide slightly unevenly.

So, when five cards are missing, declarer can expect them to divide evenly, 3-2. If six cards are missing, declarer can expect them to divide slightly unevenly, 4-2. There is no guarantee when developing tricks through length. Five missing cards could also be divided 4-1 or 5-0. Six missing cards could also be divided 3-3, 5-1, or 6-0.

FINESSE

Declarer can sometimes develop tricks with high cards when the defenders hold higher-ranking cards. One guideline is to lead toward the card you hope will take a trick. Here is an example:

DUMMY	The ♠A is a sure trick, but the ♠Q is not. The
♠ A Q	defenders have the ♠K. However, declarer can hope to take two tricks by first leading a low
DECLARER	spade toward dummy and playing—finessing—
♠ 7 6	dummy's ♠Q. If the ♠K is favorably placed on declarer's left, the ♠Q will win. If the ♠K is unfavorably placed on declarer's right, the finesse loses and declarer gets only one trick.

Here is a variation on the above example:

DUMMY
♥ Q 6 3

DECLARER
♥ A 5 4

The ♥A is a sure trick. The ♥Q might be developed into a winner if the ♥K is favorably placed on declarer's left. Declarer takes the ♥A and then leads a low heart toward dummy's ♥Q. If the ♥K is played, the ♥Q becomes a winner that can be taken later; if a low heart is played, the ♥Q will immediately win a trick. Of course, if the ♥K is unfavorably located on declarer's right, the finesse will lose and declarer will finish with only one heart trick.

Sometimes you have enough combined strength to lead a card you hope will take a trick by trapping a high card in a defender's hand. For example:

DUMMY
♦ Q J

DECLARER
♦ A 5

To get two tricks from this combination, the ♦K must be favorably placed on declarer's right. The ♦Q is led from dummy. If the ♦K is played, declarer wins the ♦A and gets a second trick with the ♦J. If the ♦K isn't played, declarer plays the ♦5. The ♦Q will win the trick if declarer's left-hand opponent doesn't hold the ♦K, and declarer gets a second trick with the ♦A.

In some situations, declarer needs to take more than one finesse in a suit. This is called a *repeated finesse*.

DUMMY
(NORTH)
♥ A Q J

DECLARER
(SOUTH)
♥ 9 4 2

Declarer could get two tricks through *promotion*, by playing the ♥A and leading the ♥Q to drive out the defenders' ♥K and promote the ♥J into a winner. If declarer needs three tricks from this suit, however, declarer will have to take two finesses.

Declarer starts by leading a low heart toward dummy and finessing the ♥J (or ♥Q). If the ♥K is favorably placed on declarer's left, the first finesse wins. Now declarer must get back to the South hand and lead another low heart toward dummy. Assuming West follows with a low heart, declarer repeats the finesse by playing dummy's ♥Q (or ♥J). Declarer can then take the ♥A for the third trick in the suit.

Notice that declarer must lead hearts twice from the South hand. This means declarer must be able to get to the South hand with a winner in another suit. A way to get from one hand to the opposite hand is called an *entry*. Declarer will need two entries to the South hand to take the repeated heart finesse. Using entries wisely is one of the important parts of considering the order when playing a deal.

Here's another example of a repeated finesse:

DUMMY
(NORTH)
♦ K Q 5

DECLARER
(SOUTH)
♦ 8 4 2

Declarer could get one trick through promotion by leading the ♦K to drive out the ♦A and promote the ♦Q into a winner. To get two tricks, declarer has to start by leading a low diamond toward dummy and playing the ♦Q or ♦K. If the ♦Q wins, declarer will need an entry in another suit to get back to the South hand and repeat the finesse by leading another low diamond toward dummy.

As long as the defender on declarer's left has the ♦A, declarer can't be prevented from developing two tricks in diamonds with the help of the repeated finesse—assuming declarer has the entries in other suits to get to the South hand twice.

There are many variations of the finesse. Finesses are discussed in more detail in the book on DECLARER PLAY.

TRUMPING IN DUMMY

In a trump contract, declarer may be able to gain a trick by using dummy's trump.

DUMMY
♥ 7 5 3
♣ 3

DECLARER
♥ A K Q J 10
♣ A 7

The trump suit is hearts. If declarer takes the five heart winners and the ♣A, declarer gets six tricks. If declarer plays the ♣A and then leads the ♣7 and trumps it in the dummy, declarer gets seven tricks: the ♣A, the *ruff*, and the five heart winners. Declarer gains a trick by trumping in the dummy.

Consider the Order

When developing and taking tricks, the order in which the tricks are played can be important. Here are some considerations:

1) Take the tricks and run. With enough sure tricks to make the contract, declarer should generally take them, before the defenders can gain the lead and take their tricks.

2) Draw trumps. In a trump contract, declarer should draw the defenders' trumps by playing the trump suit until the defenders have none left, unless declarer needs the trump suit for other purposes, such as trumping in dummy.

3) Keep enough trumps in dummy. When declarer needs extra tricks and is planning on trumping in dummy, declarer may have to delay drawing trumps. Declarer can't afford to draw so many rounds of trump that there are none left in dummy.

4) Develop extra tricks early. To develop extra tricks, one or more tricks may have to be lost to the defenders. Declarer should not be afraid to lose such tricks early in the play while keeping sure tricks in the other suits to regain the lead and then take the established winners.

5) Be in the right place at the right time. Declarer must often plan to be in the appropriate hand to take or establish winners.

6) Play the high card from the short side first. When taking sure tricks or promoting winners in suits that are unevenly divided between the two hands, it's usually a good idea to start by playing the high cards from the hand with the fewer cards.

7) Be aware of the opponents. Although declarer's primary focus is to take the number of tricks required to make the contract, declarer also needs to keep an eye on the tricks the opponents may be able to take. This is especially a concern when declarer may have to give up the lead when developing tricks. For example, suppose South is declarer in a 4♠ contract on this deal and West leads the ♥K:

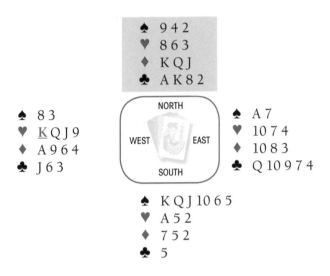

♠ 9 4 2
♥ 8 6 3
♦ K Q J
♣ A K 8 2

West:
♠ 8 3
♥ K Q J 9
♦ A 9 6 4
♣ J 6 3

East:
♠ A 7
♥ 10 7 4
♦ 10 8 3
♣ Q 10 9 7 4

South:
♠ K Q J 10 6 5
♥ A 5 2
♦ 7 5 2
♣ 5

South has one sure trick in hearts and two in clubs. South can promote five winners in spades and two more in diamonds. That's a total of ten tricks, enough to make 4♠. But look what happens if South wins the ♥A and immediately goes after the spade suit. East wins the ♠A and leads a heart. West takes two heart tricks and the ♦A. That's four tricks for the defenders and the contract is defeated.

What went wrong? The lead of the ♥K established two heart winners for the defenders to go with the ♠A and ♦A. Declarer must be aware the defenders have four tricks to take if given the lead. To prevent this, declarer has to Consider the Order. Before giving up the lead, declarer should take dummy's ♣A and ♣K, discarding a heart on the second club winner. Now it's safe to lead a spade and give up the lead. There is only one heart left in declarer's hand.

After winning the ♠A, the defenders can take one heart, but that's all. If they lead another heart, declarer can trump. The defenders get only three tricks: the ♠A, a heart, and the ♦A.

This type of consideration comes up quite frequently when playing in a contract. Declarer must become aware of the number of tricks the opponents might take if given the opportunity to gain the lead, and must decide what can be done to prevent the defenders from taking too many tricks[67].

---

[67] This is discussed in more detail in the fourth book in this series, Declarer Play.

Appendix 2 – Texas Transfers

Texas transfers are similar to Jacoby transfers but are only used when responder has a six-card or longer major suit and at least enough strength to take the partnership to the game level. After an opening bid of 1NT or 2NT[68]:

> ### Texas Transfers
>
> ↑ • A response of 4♥ is a transfer to 4♠.
> • A response of 4♦ is a transfer to 4♥.

For example:

OPENER	RESPONDER
♠ J 5	♠ K Q 10 8 7 2
♥ K Q 10	♥ 4 3
♦ K 10 5 2	♦ Q J
♣ A Q 7 5	♣ 6 4

OPENER	RESPONDER
1NT	4♥
4♠	PASS

Responder knows How High and Where the partnership belongs. By using the Texas transfer bid of 4♥, responder gets the contract played by opener, the stronger hand.

Responder could accomplish the same result by using a Jacoby transfer of 2♥, asking opener to bid 2♠, and then raising to 4♠. So there doesn't appear to be much need for Texas transfers. By using both Jacoby and Texas transfers, however, experienced partnerships can distinguish between signoff bids at the game level and slam invitations. That's beyond the scope of this series, so Texas transfers are only mentioned because they are popular in some areas.

---

[68] Or after a strong 2♣ opening, a 2♦ waiting bid by responder, and a 2NT rebid by opener.

Glossary

Advancer—The partner of a player who makes an overcall or takeout double. (page 25)

Balanced Hand—A hand with no voids, no singletons, and no more than one doubleton. (page 1)

Bidding Ladder—The order in which bids can be made, starting with 1♣ and ending with 7NT. (page 4)

Blackwood Convention—A bid of 4NT after a trump suit has been agreed to ask for the number of aces held by partner. The responses are: 5♣, 0 or 4; 5♦, 1; 5♥, 2; 5♠, 3. It is used when the partnership has enough combined strength for a slam contract but wants to check that it isn't missing too many aces. If the partnership is interested in a grand slam, a subsequent bid of 5NT asks for the number of kings held by partner. (page 143)

Bonuses—Points scored for making a partscore, game, or slam or for defeating the opponents' contract. (page 137)

Call—Any bid, double, redouble or pass. (page 40)

Cheaper Minor Negative—An artificial bid of the cheaper minor at the three level by responder to show a very weak hand of about 0–3 points after an opening bid of 2♣, a waiting response of 2♦, and a rebid of 2♥, 2♠, or 3♣ by opener. If opener bids 3♦, responder's only choice is to bid 3NT with a weak hand. (page 111)

Control—A holding in a suit which prevents the opponents from immediately taking one or two tricks. An ace, or a void in a trump contract, is a first round control, since it prevents the opponents from taking the first trick in a suit. A king, or a singleton in a trump contract, is a second round control, since it prevents the opponents from taking the first two tricks in a suit. The partnership can find out about controls through conventions such as Blackwood or Gerber, or through cuebidding. (page 145)

Conventional Bid—A bid which conveys a meaning other than what would normally be attributed to it. (page 15)

Cuebid (in the Opponent's Suit)—An artificial forcing bid in a suit bid by the opponents. It can be used by responder after an opponent overcalls and by advancer after partner overcalls. (page 33)

Cuebidding (for Slam)—Bids that show controls—aces, kings, voids, and singletons—when the partnership is interested in slam. This is an advanced topic, generally beyond the scope of this book. (page 150)

Discard—Play a non-trump card which is from a different suit than the one led. (page 53)

Distribution—The number of cards held in each suit by a particular player; the number of cards held in a particular suit by the partnership. (page 1)

Double—A call that can be used either to ask partner to bid or to increase the bonus for defeating the opponents' contract. (page 33)

Doubleton—A holding of two cards in a suit. (page 1)

Draw Trump—Playing the trump suit until the opponents have none left. (page 47)

Dummy Points—Points used in place of length points when valuing a hand in support of partner's suit: void, 5 points; singleton, 3 points; doubleton, 1 point. (page 24)

Entry—A way to get from one hand to the opposite hand. (page 49)

Finesse—A method of building extra tricks if the opponents' high card(s) are favorably located. (page 49)

First Round Control—See Control.

Fit—Ideally, three-card or longer support for a suit bid by partner. A combined partnership holding of eight or more cards in a suit will usually be a suitable trump fit. (page 3)

Forcing (Bid)—A bid that partner is not expected to pass. (page 10)

Fourth Highest—A lead of the fourth card down from the top in a suit. (page 12)

Game (Contract)—A contract which has a trick score value of 100 or more points. (page 3)

Gerber Convention—An artificial jump to 4♣ after a natural 1NT or 2NT bid to ask for the number of aces held by partner. The responses are: 4♦, 0 or 4; 4♥, 1; 4♠, 2; 4NT, 3. It is used when the partnership has enough combined strength for a slam contract, but wants to check that it isn't missing too many aces. If the partnership is interested in a grand slam, a subsequent bid of 5♣ asks for the number of kings held by partner. (page 152)

Grand Slam—A contract to take all thirteen tricks. (page 137)

HCPs—An abbreviation for high-card points. (page 1)

High Card Points—The value of high cards in a hand: ace, 4; king, 3; queen, 2; jack, 1. (page 1)

Higher-Ranking Suit—A suit that ranks higher on the Bidding Ladder than another suit. Spades are ranked highest; hearts are second; diamonds are third; clubs are the lowest-ranking suit. (page 107)

How High—The level at which the contract should be played. (page 3)

Invitational—A bid which encourages partner to continue bidding. (page 9)

Jacoby Transfers—A convention used by the responder to a 1NT opening bid when holding a five-card or longer major suit. A response of 2♦ asks opener to bid 2♥; a response of 2♥ asks opener to bid 2♠. One advantage is to have the stronger hand, the 1NT opener, as declarer in the major suit. Jacoby transfers can also be used after notrump overcalls or higher-level notrump opening bids. (page 58)

Length Points—The valuation assigned to long suits in a hand: five-card suit, 1 point; six-card suit, 2 points; seven-card suit, 3 points; eight-card suit, 4 points. (page 1)

Loser—A trick which might be lost to the opponents. (page 91)

Major (Suit)—Spades or hearts. (page 4)

Minor (Suit)—Diamonds or clubs. (page 14)

New Suit—A suit which has not previously been bid in the auction. (page 39)

Overcall—A bid made after the opponents have opened the bidding. (page 25)

Overtrick—A trick won by declarer in excess of the number required to make the contract. (page 47)

Partscore—A contract that does not receive a game bonus if made. (page 3)

Pattern—The number of cards held in each suit in a player's hand. (page 41)

Penalty—The bonus awarded to the defenders for defeating a contract. (page 35)

Penalty Double—A double made with the expectation of defeating the opponents' contract. Partner is expected to pass. (page 35)

Positive Response—A response to an artificial 2♣ opening bid other than the 2♦ waiting bid, showing about 8 or more points. (page 104)

Promotion—Developing one or more cards into winners by driving out any higher-ranking cards held by the opponents. (page 46)

Quantitative (Invitational) Raise—A raise of partner's suit or notrump bid that asks partner to continue to game or slam with maximum strength. For example, a raise of an opening bid of 1NT to 2NT asks opener to bid game with a maximum for the 1NT opening. Similarly, a raise of 1NT to 4NT would invite opener to bid slam with a maximum. (page 139)

Raise—Supporting partner's suit by bidding the suit at a higher level. (page 19)

Repeated Finesse—A finesse that may need to be taken more than once to gain one or more additional tricks. (page 49)

Responder—The partner of the opening bidder. (page 1)

Ruff(ing)—Playing a trump to a trick when holding no cards in the suit led. Same as trumping. (page 13)

Second Round Control—See Control.

Sequence—Three or more consecutive cards in a suit. (page 46)

Signoff (Bid)—A bid that asks partner to pass. (page 6)

Singleton—A holding of one card in a suit. (page 1)

Slam—A contract to take twelve or thirteen tricks. (page 3)

Small Slam—A contract to take twelve tricks. (page 137)

Stayman Convention—An artificial response of 2♣ to an opening bid of 1NT, asking if opener has a four-card major suit. With no four-card major suit, opener bids 2♦. With a four-card or five-card major suit, opener bids 2♥ or 2♠. The Stayman convention can also be used after a notrump overcall or higher-level notrump bids. (page 15)

Strong Artificial 2♣ Opening—An artificial opening bid of 2♣ to show a strong hand of about 22 or more points. (page 100)

Super-Accept—A jump by opener when replying to a Jacoby transfer bid, showing four-card support for responder's major and maximum strength. (page 58)

Support—The number of cards held in a suit that partner has bid. (page 10)

Sure Trick—A trick which can be taken without giving up the lead to the opponents. (page 47)

Texas Transfers—A similar convention to Jacoby transfers. After a 1NT or 2NT opening, a jump to 4♦ asks opener to bid 4♥; a jump to 4♥ asks opener to bid 4♠. (page 80, 215)

Trumping—Playing a trump on a trick when void in the suit led. (page 51)

Two Diamond (2♦) Waiting Bid—An artificial response of 2♦ to an opening bid of 2♣ that says nothing about responder's hand. Responder is leaving room for opener to describe the hand. (page 102)

Unbalanced Hand—A hand with a void, a singleton, or more than one doubleton. (page 14)

Unbid Suit—A suit that has not yet been bid during the auction. (page 132)

Up the Line—Bidding the cheapest of two or more four-card suits (page 15)

Valuation (Points)—A method of estimating the value of a hand during the auction, usually a combination of values for high cards and length. (page 1)

Void—A holding of zero cards in a suit. (page 1)

Waiting Bid—See Two Diamond Waiting Bid.

WHERE—The strain (clubs, diamonds, hearts, spades, or notrump) in which the contract should be played. (page 3)

Winner—A card held by one of the players that will win a trick when it is played. (page 12)

Visit our web site to get up-to-date information from Better Bridge.

www.BetterBridge.com OR www.AudreyGrant.com

PRODUCTS

Better Bridge material is prepared with the assistance of the Better Bridge Panel of world-wide experts and is available through books, disks, videos, magazines, and the Internet.

BRIDGE TEACHERS

Join the Better Bridge Teachers' Group if you are involved in bridge education. Teacher's manuals are available to assist in presenting bridge lessons to students.

CRUISES

Travel by ship, add Bridge at Sea, and you have a magic fit. Audrey Grant and the Better Bridge Team conduct bridge cruises to locations around the world.

FESTIVALS

Workshops and festivals are held in fine hotels and resorts across North America. Come with or without a partner . . . let us get a fourth for bridge.

BRIDGE QUIZ

Try the regularly updated quizzical pursuits. Test your bidding and play, spot the celebrities, and play detective at the table.

BRIDGE ONLINE

Playing bridge on the internet is becoming an increasingly popular pastime since you can play anywhere, anytime. Find out about the Audrey Grant bridge club and lessons.

CONTACT US

E-mail:	BetterBridge@BetterBridge.com
Phone:	1-888-266-4447
Fax:	1-416-322-6601
Write:	Better Bridge
	247 Wanless Avenue
	Toronto, ON M4N 1W5